War of the Ancient Dragon

War of the Ancient Dragon

TRANSFORMATION OF VIOLENCE
IN SANDPLAY

Laurel A. Howe

War of the Ancient Dragon
Transformation of Violence in Sandplay
Copyright © 2016 by Laurel A. Howe
First Edition
ISBN 978-1-77169-034-8 Paperback
ISBN 978-1-77169-035-5 eBook

Published in the United States of America by Fisher King Press. For information on obtaining permission for use of material from this work, submit a written request to:

permissions@fisherkingpress.com

Fisher King Press
www.fisherkingpress.com
+1-307-222-9575

Many thanks to all who have directly or indirectly provided permission to quote their works, including:

From *The Collected Works of C.G. Jung, Vol. 8 : The Structure and Dynamics of the Psyche* by C.G. Jung. Copyright © 1960 by Princeton University Press. Published by Princeton University Press. Reprinted by permission.

From *The Collected Works of C.G. Jung, Vol. 12 : Psychology and Alchemy* by C.G. Jung and R.F.C. Hull, translator. Copyright © 1953 by Princeton University Press. Published by Princeton University Press. Reprinted by permission.

From *The Collected Works of C.G. Jung, Vol. 13 : Alchemical Studies* by C.G. Jung and R.F.C. Hull, translator. Copyright © 1967 by Princeton University Press. Published by Princeton University Press. Reprinted by permission.

From *The Collected Works of C.G. Jung, Vol. 14 : Mysterium Coniunctionis* by C.G. Jung and R.F.C. Hull, translator. Copyright © 1963 by Princeton University Press. Published by Princeton University Press. Reprinted by permission.

Every effort has been made to trace all copyright holders; however, if any have been overlooked, the author will be pleased to make the necessary arrangements at the first opportunity.

CONTENTS

ACKNOWLEDGEMENTS

I am deeply grateful to the board members of the Centre for Research and Training in Depth Psychology According to C.G. Jung and Marie-Louise von Franz, for their devotion to original research in depth psychology. Without the examples they bring forth in their own creative work, this book, begun while a student at the Centre, would not have been possible. Ruedi Högger, Irene Gerber-Münch, and Eva Wertenschlag-Birkhäuser read early versions of the work and encouraged me to carry it further. Dr. Theodor Abt provided vital insights into the alchemical symbolism. I want to express loads of affection and gratitude to Brigitte Huber for her friendship and editorial fortitude translating a shorter version into German, and in the process helping me to see the effects of Randy's work on others. Editors Mel Mathews (Fisher King Press), Margaret Johnson and Charles Zeltzer (*Psychological Perspectives*), and Gotthilf Isler and Hansueli Etter (*Jungiana*) have had the perspective and wisdom to see in this case study the transformational capacity of a violent attitude that is allowed its symbolic voice and creative range.

I thank my children, Meril and Mo, and my husband, Matt, for their support and encouragement during work on many drafts over the years.

But especially, thank-you to Randy, whose tenacity and heart touch us and change us.

Laurel Howe
Denver, Colorado

Wherefore is this Art compared to the play of children, who when they play, turn undermost that which was uppermost.

— Solomon Trismosin, from *Splendor Solis*.

ILLUSTRATIONS

Front cover. Python (Mercurius as three-headed dragon), from the *Alchemical and rosicrucian compendium*, f. 359r. Beinecke Rare Book & Manuscript Library, Yale University.

Figure 1. Sandplay figures and a tray each of dry sand and wet sand. Author's photo.

Figure 2. Initial session, "World War I" sandtray. Author's photo.

Figure 3. Session 3, "War of the ancient dragon" sandtray. Author's photo.

Figure 4. Salamander, from Maier, *Scrutinium chymicum* (1687), p. 85.

Figure 5. Uroboric dragon with bat wings: Lambsprinck, "De lapide philosophico libellus," in *Musaeum hermeticum* (1678), p. 353.

Figure 6. Session 4, "civil war" sandtray and first burning session. Author's photo.

Figure 7. Alchemical furnace from Geber, *De alchimia libri tres* (1531), title page.

Figure 8. Descent into the alchemical bath, from *Rosarium philosophorum, secunda pars alchimiae de lapide philosophico* (1550), fig. 4, *Speculum*.

Figure 9. Alchemical pelican beakers, from Porta, G.B., *Distillationibus* (1609), p. 42.

Figure 10. King devouring his son, from Lambsprinck, "de Lapide philosophorum figurae et emblemata" in *Musaeum hermeticum* (1678), p. 367.

Figure 11. Session 5, nuclear war sandtray. Author's photo.

Figure 12. Session 11, the torture of "Hades" sandtray. Author's photo.

Figure 13. Session 12. Randy declares himself "king of the bloodfire" and smears himself with ash. Author's photo.

Figure 14. Session 12, melted candle. Author's photo.

INTRODUCTION

Six-year-old Randy walks into my office for the first time and declares, "This place smells like piss." I can't disagree with him. I have done my best to set up shop as an intern, the new and only counselor in a crowded elementary school. I occupy a musty, windowless room that used to be a supply closet. Randy is one of my first sandplay clients. Arrogant, loud, a study in ambivalence, Randy pulls no punches. He is a bad guy and wants to be known as a bad guy. In fact, Randy is a bully. He beats up his fellow first-graders and curses at his teachers. He seems to relish the attention he gets when school authorities attempt to impose "consequences" by forcing him to sit by himself in the principal's office, suspending him for days at a time, or sending him to a counselor. Nobody at the school expects sandplay therapy to help Randy much, and admittedly I have my doubts. But if therapy doesn't work, Randy will be expelled from school permanently.

Randy eyes my sandplay figures, curious in spite of himself. I tell him he can do whatever he wants with the tray (which in those days was a painted wooden box). As happens even with the most resistant children, Randy can't keep himself away from the intriguing possibility. What will he create? What story will arise? With a sidelong glance to see if he is irritating me, Randy slowly pours a large bowlful of glass jewels into the tray. Then he dumps in a bowlful of stones. He calls them "bombs." I widen my eyes and say, "that's a lot of bombs." Thus I give him tacit permission to continue. He really can do whatever he wants. Immediately he is waging a full-fledged battle. He drops people, animals, and buildings into the tray. They are bombs too. He imagines each creature exploding in a bloody eruption of sizzling fire. He embellishes the agonizing dismemberments with spit and roaring gurgles, sighs, screams, and the ooh's and ah's of someone truly impressed with the gore he is witnessing. He dubs this battle "World War I." His second session, very similar to the first, he conducts "World War II." His third battle he calls "The war of the ancient dragon." Next, he wants to light a fire.

Week after week, over the course of 24 sessions, Randy conducts battle after profoundly destructive battle. He burns fires (after much negotiation), tortures people, kills off parents, and melts entire soldiers, dooming them to harrowing deaths. As I begin to wonder if the torment and gore will ever end, he discovers something in his melted wax that is "entirely and completely new," even though it comes "from ancient times." After weeks of bullying figures in the sandtray, Randy's new-yet-ancient wax indicates that he has discovered a nascent possibility in himself—something that is ancient, but that he experiences as brand new. By then Randy has stopped his physical violence and has become engaged with school. He has gone through the better part of a miraculous transformation, ironically, through war and fire.

At the time that Randy fought the war with the ancient dragon, I had just a glimmer of an idea about what such a battle could mean psychologically. It would take more than ten years to come to a reasonably full symbolic understanding of Randy's ancient dragon and how so much war, gore, fire, agony, and dismemberment, could possibly accompany his profound healing process. As I worked over the years to amplify what he said about his trays, I began to understand that his process and his language were remarkably alchemical, sometimes calling to mind the very words of the "ancient philosopher," Zosimos.[1] Working with Randy's process, I came to understand too how sandplay actually *is* alchemy.

Sandplay and Alchemy

C.G. Jung's journey into the unconscious began through a kind of sandplay. In 1912, feeling disoriented after his break from Freud, Jung found himself occupied with childhood memories and engrossed in a "rite" of building imaginary villages on the bank of Lake Zürich using rocks, sand, mud, and water. For months he felt compelled to play this way

---

1   I will be referring to "The Visions of Zosimos" in C.G. Jung's *Alchemical Studies*, CW 13. Note: CW refers throughout this publication to the Collected Works of C.G. Jung.

in order to engage his memories and creative impulses in a completely spontaneous way. He reports in his autobiography:

> Naturally, I thought about the significance of what I was doing, and asked myself, "Now really, what are you about? You are building a small town, and doing it as if it were a rite!" I had no answer to my question, only the inner certainty that I was on the way to discovering my own myth. For the building game was only a beginning. It released a stream of fantasies which I later carefully wrote down.
>
> This sort of thing has been consistent with me, and at any time in my later life when I came up against a blank wall, I painted a picture or hewed stone. Each such experience proved to be a *rite d'entrée* for the ideas and works that followed hard upon it.[2]

Jung came to describe his imaginal work as a form of active imagination, a meditative and creative participation of the conscious mind with images and energies that arise of their own accord from the unconscious. Imaginal activity in the form of play, artwork, writing, or meditation can take an adult back to the playlike world of childhood via a lowering of the mental functioning level, to a state in which the imagination is released from the usual conscious restraints, and the ego is free to roam in unconscious images. An adult enters the imaginal realm with the goal of engaging the unconscious. A child just enters, following his natural impulse. Although the child is not conscious of a goal, the psyche is.

The waking experience of psychic images comes with varying degrees of intensity, ranging from the engaged play with imaginary figures that Jung describes, to focused meditation and active imagination, to involuntary visions, some of which can be overwhelming to modern consciousness. Jung reported his own experiences with visions in his autobiography and transcribed them in his *Red Book*.[3] Because he had engaged

---

2 C.G. Jung, *Memories, Dreams, Reflections*, pp. 174-5. Note: *MDR* refers throughout this publication to C.G. Jung's *Memories, Dreams, Reflections*.
3 C.G. Jung, *The Red Book: Liber Novus*.

in his own "confrontation with the unconscious,"[4] when years later Jung discovered alchemical texts, he could identify alchemical work as a form of active imagination. What the alchemists called their *meditatio,* Jung identified as "an inner dialogue and hence a living relationship to the answering voice of the 'other' in ourselves, i.e., of the objective psyche."[5] Alchemists saw in their retorts salamanders, dragons, spirits, and Mercurius, among other things—in part projected manifestations of unconscious psychic energy. We will see how such imaginal images guide a process of transformation as we move through Randy's sessions and amplify in detail his own dragons, soldiers, and other spirits.

Randy's war, his fire, the figures in the sandtray happen to be remarkably alchemical in their motifs. But these motifs *per se* are not what make his sandplay alchemical. Rather, the imaginative phenomenon, in which inner psychic material is projected into the retort of the sandtray and worked, makes sandplay an alchemical *opus.* Sandplay is a form of active imagination in which psychological dynamics spontaneously come forward to be experienced as outer, objective reality and converse with ego consciousness. In Randy's work we have a chance to observe the details of such a conversation, in which consciousness and the unconscious are fully engaged with each other. It is important for us to understand that the therapeutic *containment* of Randy's violent urges is also critical. For an adult, containing an urge while doing active imagination entails a deliberate suppression of that urge, toward a transformative goal. For Randy, the containment is provided by the sandtray, and the therapeutic situation, including the transference and counter-transference. I am conscious that his violent urge is being contained, and I know that my psyche and his psyche together are engaged in this containment.[6] Randy's psyche may know that something important is happening. Randy himself comes to his play in all seriousness, as if he were on a mission.

---

4   The title of a chapter in Jung's autobiography, *Memories, Dreams, Reflections.*

5   C.G. Jung, *Psychology and Alchemy,* CW 12, ¶ 390.

6   Many sandplay therapists use Kay Bradway's term, "co-transference" to refer to the psychic energy and cooperation that occurs in the transference and counter-transference, and includes the sandplay material and activity. See Bradway and McCoard, *Sandplay: Silent Workshop of the Psyche.*

But he doesn't necessarily understand that the containment of his violent urge imbues the imaginal situation in the sandtray with the energy required for transformation to occur. Randy's imagination projects his violent urges and his inner dragon into the sandtray, where he experiences them as "other." He may not consciously reflect on his sandplay work as an inner phenomenon, but nevertheless, it has an effect on him. Randy's narrative illustrates in detail how his own psychological transformation occurs in the imaginal realm, through an archetypal drama on which his life depends.

Because children have an immediate and spontaneous relationship to the unconscious, what they do in play and what they say about their play gives us a chance to observe at close range the contents and process of the unconscious in the contemporary psyche as it moves through its own healing range. Randy's narrative is his own, but his words and actions—his operations—connect him to the alchemy of the ages via his symbolic process. Like an alchemist, the child is a naïve participant in his work with the psyche. In a child's play we see an individuation process, not one that is engaged by a mature ego, but one that occurs in a natural way, uninterrupted by the typically analytical and skeptical consciousness of an adult. In this natural way, the child is more like an alchemist than the adult—he projects something into matter without hesitation, expecting something important to happen.

The violence that lives in Randy as volatile energy (the dragon) becomes materialized. In other words, it is given a place to project itself, a place to live out its own, inherent narrative, in the realm of the imaginal world, within the safe container of the sandtray and sandplay therapy. Randy's violent attitude, rooted in conflict on the archetypal level, is projected into the tray and "worked" over and over. It moves through stages and gradually clarifies itself. Nobody interferes with this process; it is never criticized or analyzed, and it doesn't need to be. It only needs containment that acknowledges its transpersonal context. Gradually the violent energy begins to transform, and as it does, it loosens its grip on Randy: this is the miracle we watch in Randy's trays. Fire transforms fire. Violence transforms violence. The transformation taking place in the retort of the sandtray is a projection of an inner phenomenon. Simultaneously, spontaneously, the transformation takes place in

Randy's personality. When the "ancient dragon" appears in Randy's tray, that dragon tells us that Randy is engaging the full participation of the imaginal realm. He can see his own fiery nature as if it were a chthonic being from an ancient world.

Sandplay Overview

Sandplay as a form of analytical psychotherapy was established by Dora Kalff, a Swiss woman who studied with C.G. Jung.[7] Jung suggested that Kalff develop a psychological method for working with children and made her aware of Freudian psychoanalyst Margaret Lowenfeld's World Technique, in which children were allowed to play with objects in a sandtray in order to present a conscious, life situation. Jung and Kalff saw that the unconscious also was present in the tray, the symbolic dimension coming to life. With this insight Kalff developed her method of sandplay.[8]

A sandplay therapist has a tray of dry sand and a tray of wet sand (Figure 1). The tray is just large enough so you can see its entire contents without moving your eyes. Numerous figures on the therapist's shelves represent the world—the outer world but of course also the inner world.[9] Each session, the client can put anything they want in the tray, or simply form the sand. The goal is to play, to lower the level of consciousness so that the psychological situation can come forward through a deep engagement of the imagination. Sometimes the sandplayer only wants to handle the sand, other times an elaborate story will form spontaneously and the tray will fill with figures and objects from everyday life or from nature. With adults, some amplification may take place after a tray is formed, as if working with a dream, to bring the ego into stronger connection with the image. Amplification—a way of bringing the symbols to life with associations from life or mythology—

---

7 See Dora Kalff, *Sandplay: A Psychotherapeutic Approach to the Psyche*.

8 "Sandplay" therapy is distinct from "sandtray" therapy, which is practiced as a form of generic (non-Jungian) play therapy, generally not taking the symbolic realm into account.

9 Barbara Turner's *Handbook of Sandplay Therapy* provides case studies and a thorough guide for methods and materials.

may vary from therapist to therapist, and client to client. With children, no interpretation is done during or after the session at all; doing so would break through the healing, imaginal world. Dora Kalff exhorted sandplay therapists to allow the child to lead the way, to allow the imagination to develop its own narrative, and when the process might seem strange or even destructive, to "let it be," refraining from judgement or guidance.

Figure 1. Sandplay therapists offer shelves full of figures and a tray each of dry sand and wet sand. Trays are typically lined with blue to represent water, or the depths.

Children and adults sometimes dream about their trays, another indication that their sandplay work is stirring the unconscious. An adult encounter with the psyche in the sandtray can open up an ongoing dialogue on its own, or in the context of an analysis. Sandplay can help foster a feeling connection with the reality of the psyche, so critical to individuation.

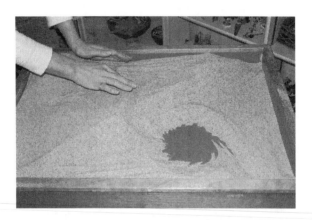

Dry sand tray.

Wet sand tray.

Chapter 1

WORLD WAR ONE: CAN YOU IMAGINE?

In his first encounter with the sandtray (Figure 2) Randy knows exactly what he wants to do. Into the tray, without hesitating or asking permission, he pours a bowlful of glass jewels he calls bombs. He adds a bowlful of stones. Everything explodes dramatically. He adds sound effects, and his spittle-crackling, throat-gurgling eruptions signal the indiscriminate deaths of any creature that gets in the way. Soldiers, snakes, R2D2, trucks, stones, dragons, jewels, everything that enters the tray is either a bomb or destroyed by a bomb. He revels in the destruction, and relishes the foamy sounds with which he articulates the bloody dismemberment of his victims.

A black panther (lower center) at one point takes the part of the protagonist, and Randy says, "There are so many people trying to kill this guy. He's gonna get shot in the heart." The panther is shot in the heart, and the panther's baby is shot, rolling through the air and landing face down in the sand. "It's like World War I," Randy says. "Can you imagine?"

I try to imagine what, for a six-year-old boy, World War I could possibly feel like. He has come to the tray and without hesitation, self-consciousness, or shame, and has shown me his first concern. Randy asks me to witness, but further, to imagine, the "first" war within him. A first war could be the fundamental psychic war, the archetypal war, within Randy. It could be the first stage of the alchemical hostile situation, the *massa confusa,* the basic conflict in him that threatens his experience of himself as a valid reality in the world. A world war is a war between the opposites on the archetypal level, and Randy is somehow caught there, between those violent opposing forces. In Randy's war the difference between good and bad is missing or ambivalent: the protagonist is shot in the heart, the central region of the personality, his basic experience of himself.

Figure 2. Initial session, "World War I." Although the tray is decidedly chaotic, an incipient circular formation indicates a vague orientation around the center. Elements from future trays already appear here, including the father and baby bears and the stone heart in the center of the tray.

Jung writes that symbols and experiences of the opposites, such as those that are expressed in war:

> do not belong to the ego personality but are supraordinate to it. The ego personality occupies an intermediate position, like the "anima inter bona et mala sita" (soul placed between good and evil). The pairs of opposites constitute the phenomenology of the paradoxical *self,* man's totality. That is why the sym-

bolism makes use of cosmic expressions like *coelum / terra.*
The intensity of the conflict is expressed in symbols like fire
and water, height and depth, life and death.[1] (Italics Jung's.)

Randy, like many children, experiences the "intensity of conflict"
directly, without the help of a more mature ego that can realize the
archetypal dimension of the conflict and gain any separation from it.
Any child expressing conflict in terms of cosmic opposites is dealing
with dynamics that are way beyond his or her ego's capacity to negoti-
ate. Because he is only six years old, Randy has a very thin membrane
between his ego and the war of opposites. On a daily basis he lives the
intensity of a conflict that is deeply rooted in his psyche. Knowing this,
we can understand that the conflict requires a creative, imaginal outlet
in which it can work itself out according to its own nature, so it can
begin to lessen its grip on Randy as a battleground. It is impossible for
him to contain the conflict, or to exercise much choice, until the archetypal material *itself* is provided with some kind of a container in which
it can be resolved.

A protagonist getting shot in the heart is one of the first events of
Randy's sandplay process. This is telling, because the heart will play a
key role in his healing process. A wounded heart is a wound in the
feeling capacity, leaving an inadequate ability to value oneself or others. Being shot in the heart, having a destroyed capacity to relate, is a
prerequisite to any condition in which a person would engage in violent
behavior. Randy exhibits a damaged feeling capacity in his ambivalent
relationship to good and evil, as would anyone suffering violent urges.
This ambivalence is the nature of an archetypal conflict, like the one
that posesses Randy when he is fighting a "world" war. Archetypes have
an absolute quality about them and are not related to the human values of good and evil. The effect of this conflict on the ego level is that
Randy doesn't identify with the humanly "good" or moral aspect of the
conflict. Randy himself doesn't know whether he is good or bad; ego
development on this level has failed. He is telling me further that he
does not experience himself as a person with a moral choice, a basically
good person. He is a product of conflict, some of it archetypal, some of

---

1   C.G. Jung, *Mysterium Coniunctionis*, CW 14, ¶ 4.

it personal, and he is identified with that conflict instead of the good guy, or the good, adapted ego. Randy's task is in separating himself from this conflict so he can find his true feeling towards himself and compassion for others. When the contaminated, black condition of the conflict (the *nigredo,* perhaps personified by the black panther) is brought into the tray, there is a potential for the archetypal conflict to be fought out, and the ego's identification with conflict to be extracted.

Drawing on the work of Erich Neumann, Dora Kalff refers to the "fighting stage" in every child's development as a normal process in which the ego fights its way out of the parental container to achieve a certain level of independence.[2] At Randy's age, children fight to form a conscious identity, an ego, out of their younger, less organized personalities and the background of inherited influences. Each child gradually develops and identifies with the unique personality into which he or she was born through a natural process of individuation. For some children, individual development can take the form of an intensive battle, especially if their family circumstances or inner conflict threaten or obstruct their sense of individuality. At the age of six, Randy is at the perfect age for such a war, but he is not emerging as a hero; there are no good guys in his wars, and his protagonist gets shot through the heart. Randy is contained in and driven by war. He has become identified with the fight.

Personal and Impersonal Fate

Looking into Randy's personal life helps us to understand his intense hostility, but not with the expectation of an exclusive, cause-and-effect explanation. Each child is born with his own "intermediate position" in the phenomenology of the opposites, that is, in his own fateful experience of the dynamic and paradoxical Self. Randy's parents divorced when he was two and a half. They continue to live in open hostility towards each other, often expressing that hostility to Randy. Sometimes they even use Randy as a weapon, planting information on him that will explode in the other parent's face. He has experienced himself as a living

---

2   Neumann divides the stages into "magic-warlike" and "solar-warlike" as described in *The Child,* p.139. Kalff discusses the fighting stage throughout her book, *Sandplay.*

bomb. As a result, Randy lives with an intense insecurity in himself, his parents, and his world. Arrogance and violence make up his defensive front.

These personal circumstances help explain how in Randy's war "these guys just explode," or how "there are so many people trying to kill this guy," the protagonist. But the impersonal aspect of the situation must also be considered. The "intermediate position" into which Randy was born is circumstantially his position between warring parents. Their war, in turn, is an aspect of a collective war, the battle of psychic opposites. Randy experiences the archetypal situation through his parents, and through his parents his ego has become overburdened with war. Of course, I talk to Randy's parents and try to make them more conscious of the effect their hostility has on their son. Like all parents, they do not consciously want to hurt their child. After our discussion, they are more aware of how their behavior effects Randy. But we cannot expect the parents' new awareness alone to heal Randy. One can only hope that a bit of consciousness in them will help soften the extent to which Randy has to live out his parents' unconscious situation.

Talking to the parents helps them engage more consciously in strengthening Randy's ego, which is so important if he is to have a chance to deal with inner and outer conflict. I also encourage Randy to describe what it is like to get angry and hit someone, and to imagine what it feels like to be hit by him. We have to consider that most adults, let alone children, do not have the verbal capacity to describe a dynamic emotional state, especially while they are in it. But when a child cannot control his emotional energy as would be expected for his age, we must do everything we can to help him consciously contain that energy. Asking a child to describe what is going on in his body when he cannot contain his emotions can sometimes help him take a stand against the compulsion he experiences. If he can express himself, or describe even what he just did when he was in an emotional state, this can help his ego strengthen in the face of the emotion. Otherwise, he is in danger of being overcome by the destructive aspect of the energy, and his ego cannot fully form out of the emotional dynamics. It is not Randy's fault that he is a bully, yet he does cooperate with the urge and, at the moment, sees no need to resist it.

In *The Feminine in Fairy Tales*, Marie-Louise von Franz reminds us that children encounter inner as well as outer forces that challenge the ego to develop out of its inherited, and infantile state:

> If you look at the unconscious processes of children, you will see that there are play impulses, dreams and fantasies that tend to bring forth the maturity the child should have. So you could say that it is the unconscious which wants the improvement in the ego. The infantile ego does not want it. It is the impulse from the unconscious that causes the neurotic disturbance in its attempts to get the child on to a higher level of consciousness, to build up a stronger ego-complex. The school technique—being able to concentrate and overcome fatigue—is inadequate without the instinct from the unconscious, which expresses the tendency for building up such things. Therefore the urge is a general human disposition, i.e., archetype, which comes forth from the Self.[3]

Randy's violence, paradoxically, is an instinct from the unconscious, an archetype, pushing him for an improvement, a maturity, that he hasn't yet been able to achieve. On the one hand it seems to threaten the ego, and so far it has gotten Randy into trouble. On the other hand it offers a transformational path not imaginable from the outer, rational world. It seems that Randy was born into and infected with violence. He has become identified with it, and now must take on the responsibility of facing it.

Later in the same chapter, von Franz compares the personal and archetypal aspects of an individual's psychological fate to the particle and wave aspects of light. Are we cursed or blessed, or do we bring our fates on ourselves? Von Franz says both are true. She is discussing the fairy tale, "Sleeping Beauty" or "Briar Rose."

> Why does Briar Rose come under such a terrible curse [to sleep for 100 years]? One version says it is a just-so story, and the other version, that the goddess was angry because she had been ignored. There may have been real uncertainty about the problem. It is like the modern theory of light. One theory

---

3   M.L. von Franz, *The Feminine in Fairy Tales*, p. 16.

has it that light is made up of particles, the other that it is in waves. It would seem that if one is true, the other could not be. Similarly, either neurosis is caused through some transgression and cured by an ethical change of attitude or it is bad luck caused by nature and changed by good luck. Each view excludes the other, yet apparently both are true. One should see the double aspect and treat the neurosis from both sides, even though the aspects radically contradict one another.[4]

Randy's curse is his hostility, yet underneath that hostility is a sleeping, unconscious feeling capacity that slips farther away from ego consciousness as Randy acts out his aggression. We can see how a world war expresses the bad luck of being born into a hostile family or a warlike psychic situation. But Randy also participates in transgressions that exacerbate his situation. In hitting his fellow students or cursing at his teachers, his ego only becomes more and more infected with the archetypal conflict. It is imperative to recognize the "transgressions," if we can call them that in a child, for their healing aim. It is wrong to hit one's classmates, and I work with Randy to deal with his impulses consciously. This helps build up ego strength and a conscious sense of responsibility regarding his own actions. When I ask him to imagine what it would be like to be hit by someone as strong as he, I try to help build consciousness of the violence, and it allows some inkling of his inner compassion to filter through to consciousness. But if we only deal with the transgressions on a behavioral level and fail to see the archetypal war welling up from *within* Randy, we feed his experience of helplessness in the throes of his violent fate. We ask him to make a change by will power alone, and over-estimate the ability of the ego to contain the enormous dynamism of his inner war. Like a neurosis in an adult, violent acts in a child are the psyche's way of calling for recognition. If recognized as such, those violent acts, and the warring attitude in Randy, can return him to his true nature. In alchemical terms, when the stone, which is an allegorical reference to the individual personality, comes forward in its current, contaminated state, the stone can transform. The stone in its contaminated state is Randy's identification with bullying and power. In sandplay we work with that identification directly. The

4   von Franz, *The Feminine in Fairy Tales*, p. 26.

emotional energies that cling to identification and define identification are expressed nonverbally, directly, creatively. The emotional energy is objectified, separated from the child during the play and projected into the sandplay experience. That emotion then finds the natural medium for its own transformation. Getting the dynamism into the sandtray in the first place accomplishes a level of separation: the child is outside the tray, the emotional content is inside the tray. The "people trying to kill this guy" in the sandtray no longer live solely within Randy but are projected into the tray where they can be experienced as objective realities, and transform. Their energy transforms. Over time, Randy completes a detailed separation from the warlike energy that has possessed him, and that energy itself is worked. In the end, Randy is able to contain the transformed energy and develops more ethical, feeling-oriented choices regarding his behavior. Our unlikely guide in this transformation process is the "ancient dragon," who appears in his third session.

Chapter 2

WAR OF THE ANCIENT DRAGON

In his third session, Randy conducts another frightfully destructive war involving a dragon, snakes, vehicles, gems, and airplanes (Figure 3). He says,

> They've had ten wars already. Do you know how many have been shot and killed? A hundred and thirty-five good guys, just as many bad guys, and as many snakes and dragons as you see. If you even touch the dragon, you blow up. There is so much fire in them that these guys just blow up. This little thing [a glass jewel] is going to make a huge explosion. Everything is dying.

And then, in spite of himself, Randy says something hopeful:

> Only one guy survived because he didn't have an explosion in him. They made him to be a real human, and he's only half-dead.

And then this little boy says,

> It was the war of the ancient dragon. It was twelve hundred million years before you were ever alive.

Figure 3. Session 3, "war of the ancient dragon." One guy survives and is "made into a real human," though is not in the tray. The dragon is in the right side of the pile of destruction, upside down with wheels showing.

Although Randy plays in the present moment, on the psychic level he also fights an ancient war that takes place in the timelessness of the collective unconscious, "twelve hundred million years before you were ever alive." By "you," Randy seems to be referring to everyone and no one. He is talking to himself, and to me, to anyone who will listen. Randy's dramatic language calls up the deep past of his imaginal world, the world in which his war exists, linking now with then, personal with transpersonal, consciousness with the collective unconscious. In one sense, by saying "you," Randy is talking to me, to my unconscious psyche. He is saying that through the transference and counter-transference, I am part of the ongoing drama, and I'd better realize how ancient, how archetypal, it really is. In the sessions I do feel this ancient quality. I feel how important these wars are to Randy, to our relationship, and even to the psyche itself, which we observe in the raw truth of its savage opposites.

Randy is completely engaged in his war, in the destruction, the death, the dismemberment, the brutality. The goal at the moment seems to be destructive, even indulgently so; people and animals are burned, tortured, and killed. On the one hand, the devilish nature of Randy's wars belongs to his personal experience of himself and the world—he plays out the anger and violence that brought him to therapy. But the destructive urge also belongs to the autonomous psyche, and as such, has a healing aim. Randy's naming this war after the ancient dragon is an indication of this autonomous presence, which is dangerous, but also can renew. The appearance of the ancient, archetypal dragon thus reveals a paradoxical healing indicator from the depths of Randy's psyche, and signals cautious hope.

The dragon is the ancient animal unconscious still writhing in us. It is a collective chthonic energy, an archetypal phenomenon of unrealized proportions. We see the dragon in its gripping emotionality fueling war and discord around the world, and in our lives at home. We each have our personal manifestation of the dragon: a torturous longing, a persistent addiction, a haunting memory or temptation, a recurring depression, or a painful identification with a wound. The dragon is the just-so affliction of the fate to which we are born. For Randy the dragon emerges as a tenaciously violent and deprecating attitude towards his classmates, teachers, and himself. It has come forward now, and can be seen, exposed to the light of consciousness. Once the dragon-like complex is engaged and contained in a creative enterprise, its positive side may emerge. The profoundly negative and profoundly positive aspects of the dragon are identical to those of the spirit Mercurius, who dwells within the indestructible stone of the personality and secretly promotes individuation.

Imagination as the Star in Man

In Randy's "war of the ancient dragon," violence has found a theriomorphic expression. The dragon appears as a fiery phenomenon that causes explosions and dismemberment in the sandtray. As I mentioned in the introduction, it isn't the dragon itself that makes Randy's sandplay alchemical; it is the imaginal work that makes his play and narrative alchemical. In this sense every sandplay process is alchemical, but Randy's dragon and later his fire lend a peculiarly alchemical atmosphere to his work that opens a window for us to peek into the alchemical nature of the transformative imagination.

In *Psychology and Alchemy*, Jung makes it clear that some alchemists actually did see images like dragons appear in their retorts, an effect of a deeply religious, concentrated approach to the *opus*. Jung realized that the alchemist projected his own psychic material into the retort and experienced it as a creature. The reality in the retort was at least part psychic. Whether factually material or not, the creature appearing in the retort was "the result of the mind's working on matter."[20] The ability to see a dragon, salamander (Figure 4), homunculus (Figure 21), or spiritual being in the retort may seem a bit overblown until we remember how real our imaginary monsters seemed when we were children, or when we watch a child completely engaged in sandplay. We could call these imaginary events the result of projection, and we would be correct. We get in trouble when we call imaginary events "just" projection, as if projection were an immaterial or inconsequential phenomenon that can be whisked away or "cured." In fact projection is a powerful event that can enable us to become familiar with the inner workings of our souls, in sometimes tedious, sometimes profound ways.

When our own psychic content is projected onto someone else, we experience that projection as a fact. When you see, for example, a critical attitude projected onto someone, you see that attitude as belonging to the other person. And indeed, you have to say it is a fact; it is a true, psychic fact, a personal experience, even partly an objective one—you are seeing what is projected "out there" as much as from "in here." When Randy projects his denigrating shadow onto a classmate, he really does experience the classmate as worthless, but Randy also has an experience of his own self-denigration. His projection is a fact that causes a reaction in him. But it is an unconscious fact, tied to a certain emotional quality and a set of thoughts which nearly completely posess him.

When he puts that denigrating, explosive experience into the sandtray, Randy sees it there as well, and violence in the sandtray is just as much a factual experience as it is in the world. But in the sandtray the violent experience is contained in a creative dialogue outside Randy, and in containment this volatile energy can can be transformed—that is, its spirit and soul can be extracted and worked. So what he sees in the tray

---

20 Jung, *Psychology and Alchemy,* CW 12, ¶ 377.

and works with is the animating, volatile energy of his hostility—the dragon. He sees and experiences the spirit of the dragon, as it exists in the material of his personality, but he sees it as an external, objective reality. Likewise the alchemist's salamander, though projected, is an objective reality, reflecting what is happening in the alchemist. The dragon or the salamander is also a third reality between the alchemist and the stone, a living quality that exists by virtue of their imaginal dialogue. Who's to say that dragon isn't a discrete, material phenomenon? It lives by virtue of the imagination, and it has its own effect. It is an autonomous event, so to call it a projection is only partly correct. If Randy sees the ancient war of the dragon, I believe him. I also believe that this experience of the dragon is itself an answering voice from the objective psyche that is leading us to the next step in Randy's transformation.

If Randy were an alchemist he would be trying to extract from his hostile dragon its own animating energy—its spirit and its soul, or its mental aspects. The spirit and soul as our mental aspects in very basic terms represent thinking and feeling, or a certain mode of consciousness and its emotional component. Seeing the dragon in the tray in the first place puts Randy in direct contact with that animating, mental energy—his mentality. He recognizes it when he says, "this is the monster for today." The monster is the energy of the violent attitude, and by working it and burning it he extracts the mysterious animating quality in the hostility that grips him and of its own accord projects itself onto others. Each session, Randy works with a different aspect of this monster, this dragon, the chthonic autonomous unconsciousness of his mental affliction. As he works with it in the tray, it becomes volatilized, as we shall see, slowly revealing itself, clarifying itself, and loosening its grip on Randy; it is a spiritual as much as a material process, affecting Randy's attitude and his experience of himself and the world. The meaning of the dragon changes through the process, and in turn changes Randy in every way.

The salamander in the fire or the dragon in the sandtray is a living entity that indicates the beginning of a spiritualization: the image provides the evidence that the animating spirit and the yearning soul have been extracted and can now participate in the work at hand rather than remain in the dark matter of the unconscious situation. When you can take a torturous urge like violence and contain it in the heated vessel of your imagination and ask it what it wants, you extract from it a spirit, that is, a bit of consciousness, as well as its emotional yearning quality, its soul. The energy experienced in projection at the beginning can eventually be realized as one's own "mental state," a spiritual essence linked to a particular yearning.

The distinction between spirit and body, psyche and matter, was not so clear for the medieval alchemist as it is for us. Not knowing about the chemical behavior of certain materials, the alchemist saw in matter a mysterious, autonomous, divine spirit that seemed to motivate matter to behave certain ways. Imagine experiencing sulfur's strange odor and animated, volatile behavior without knowing about its chemical makeup. The alchemist was trying to elicit from the sulfur the godlike essence that makes it smoke, steam, stink, and transform. But through projection, as Jung recognized, the alchemist also elicited the spirit that moves *himself*, first contaminated, and then clarified through a lengthy process of purification and extraction.

Jung, for example, documents an unknown French alchemist who saw the salamander (a form of the dragon, Figure 4) in the fire of the retort. The alchemist reported this vision as an indication that the ancient philosophers who came before him were pleased with his work:

> How often did their pleasure in the wonderful discoveries I
> made concerning the abstruse doctrines of the ancients move
> them to reveal unto my eyes and fingers the Hermetic vessel,
> the salamander, the full moon and the rising sun.[21]

The French alchemist describes the experience of seeing and even touching animated visions in the retort as a phenomenal achievement of the imagination. His work is witnessed by "the ancients," previous alchemists and their wisdom. As Jung emphasized, the alchemists worked to uncover the original, animating spirit of the world, the *unus mundus,* the thought of God, the way God imagined the world before the world materialized.[22] This animating spirit was named many things

21   Jung, *Psychology and Alchemy*, CW 12, ¶ 391.
22   See also von Franz, "Symbols of the Unus Mundus," *Psyche and Matter* pp. 40-41.

in alchemy, among them the dragon, the stone, and Mercurius. The experience of a vision as material reality outside, revealed to the fingers as well as to the eyes, corresponds to the fact and the intensity of psychic activity in the context of the archetypal realm. Transformation occurs not only in the vessel cooking in the fire "out there," but also in the alchemist himself, for what he sees is at least partly a projection of his own meditation, his psychic content. The work in the vessel has an effect on the alchemist, and an image of that effect appears before him. The new image in turn effects him, and a continuing process of mutual transformation is engaged. We can see this phenomenon taking place in Randy: his violence appears before him in his sandplay and has an effect on him. The effect it has on him appears again in the next tray, but it is changed because he has had an effect on the violence. Rather than get projected onto a classmate, Randy's violent attitude gets projected onto the sandplay images, and there it lives as an active, material phenomenon with which Randy can interact. He is separated from it while he works with it, and can experience it as the energic, autonomous entity that it is. He works with the animated and animating essence of the violence. In his retort he sees and works with that essence *per se*. In the war, and later, fire, Randy works with the dark spirit of the violence, even as it occurs in the collective unconscious. He witnesses the chthonic dragon, the untransformed god, calling out for redemption in human consciousness. Randy does his work for himself, but like every good alchemist, he contributes the result of his work to the collective; in the end he has a certain awareness of how his transformed nature changes the world around him.

The appearance of an image as a reality can also be called a vision, like the religious visions of Niklaus von Flue, or St. Theresa, or Carl Jung. Such visions are sometimes welcome, sometimes not. A vision is an intense experience of the psyche, containing so much energy that the content of the psychic reality crosses the border into material reality and says, "I am both. I am psyche and I am matter. I am inside you and I am outside you." A vision is not a trivial experience for the sane nor for the insane, and brings with it an unusual insight into the living reality of the archetypal psyche and the meaning it tries to convey. If you have ever felt the impact of a vision, you know that it has both energy and a material quality. It may be a phenomenon of what Jung calls the psychoid realm.[23]

Figure 4. "The Mercurial spirit of the *prima materia*, in the shape of a salamander, frolicking in the fire."—Maier, The appearance of the salamander, the moon or the rising sun indicates that the alchemist's *meditatio*, the "mind working on matter," is bringing forth the animating spirit of Mercurius in its reptilian aspect.

---

23   An archetype is a form of psychic energy that can take the shape of an image in dreams, myths, or visions. It is a shapeshifter that can find its home anywhere. The archetype *per se* is pure psychic energy without form and with no humanly pre-determined meaning, though it may have a history of images. Hellenistic gods, for example, are not archetypes *per se*, but religious images stemming from archetypal energy that was constellated a certain way in Hellenistic times. The archetype *per se* is eternal and ultimately unknowable to the time-bound mind; the archetypal *image* can be seen, even smelled or touched in a vision and is known to some extent, but changes depending on our relationship with it.

Jung quotes from and discusses Ruland's *Lexicon alchemiae* in which the alchemist defines *meditatio* as a living relationship with the psyche, not only a function of the head but of the soul:

> "The word *meditatio* is used when a man has an inner dialogue with someone unseen. It may be with God, when He is invoked, or with himself, or with his good angel"... The psychologist is familiar with this "inner dialogue"; it is an essential part of the technique for coming to terms with the unconscious. Ruland's definition proves beyond all doubt that when the alchemists speak of *meditari* they do not mean mere cogitation, but explicitly an inner dialogue and hence a living relationship to the answering voice of the "other" in ourselves, i.e., of the unconscious. The use of the term "meditation" in the Hermetic dictum "And as all things proceed from the One through the meditation of the One" must therefore be understood in this alchemical sense as a creative dialogue, by means of which things pass from an unconscious potential state to a manifest one. Thus we read in Philalethes: "**Above all it is marvelous that our stone, although already perfect and able to impart a perfect tincture, does voluntarily humble itself again and will meditate a new volatility...**" What is meant by a "meditated volatility" we discover a few lines lower down, where it says, "Of its own accord it will liquefy... and by God's command become endowed with spirit, which will fly up and take the stone with it." Again, therefore, to "meditate" means that through a dialogue with God yet more spirit will be infused into the stone, i.e., it will become more spiritualized, volatilized, or sublimated."[24] (Bold mine.)

The essential mystery of alchemy, sandplay, or any form of depth psychology is that the psyche, "does voluntarily humble itself" to transform. This statement seems to refer to the autonomous and objective nature of the unconscious psyche, which voluntarily appears to converse with consciousness, via the imagination, in projection, dreams, visions, sandplay, artwork, etcetera. In projection and in fate the psyche appears whether bidden or unbidden, but we cannot necessarily will

---

24 Jung, *Psychology and Alchemy*, CW 12, ¶¶ 390-391, bold mine.

a psychic vision to appear if we are not reverent enough towards the phenomenon. The French alchemist is very happy when the salamander or the full moon or the rising sun appears, because this appearance of the basic animating principle of matter, the spirit Mercurius, rewards him for his attention, indicating that he has found the right meditative attitude towards the *opus*. If he does not have the right approach, nothing appears. The same is true for anyone if we cannot find the right approach to our own imaginations: the psyche will not volunteer itself for a conversation; it will not become animated.

Randy naturally has the right meditative attitude towards the violence. He takes it seriously and experiences its autonomy—its spirit and soul— as realities. It would not be the right attitude to take a power approach toward the violence and try to eliminate it. Rather, Randy's serious play finds the answering voice hidden in the violence itself, by isolating it in his meditative, creative process. He contains the vast emotional energy in his hostility and asks what *it* wants—a task more difficult than it sounds for many adults. As Jung states in the quote above, through the "creative dialogue...things pass from a potential state to a manifest one." Randy as a child already has the right attitude: he puts the violence into the retort of the sandtray and lets the violence speak its own language. The violence then puts itself through a protracted transformation process in which it suffers its own torture. An adult might have a more difficult time letting complexes speak for themselves, but when an adult can allow this to happen, he or she can engage in an imaginative process in which the complexes are personified and make their aims more clear. The inner potential state thus finds a way to become manifested out of the unconscious situation. You can easily imagine what you want; it is a different experience to realize that through your imagination your psyche is telling you something you really didn't know, even something you can't yet accept. You have to take the complex seriously and listen to what *it* says, which may seem completely unintelligible and probably is paradoxical, as Randy's play shows us. But taking the complex seriously is the only way to hear the answering voice of the inner other and clarify the aim of the complex.

When a complex becomes clarified enough, when you've accepted what you thought you could not about yourself, there comes a moment

when you experience the complex as an objective phenomenon that has
its own meaning and intention, which is to enlarge consciousness. You
are no longer inside the complex, blinded and contained by the object
of your desire. You have enough distance to see what the complex is and
how it effects you, from a perspective that is larger than that afforded by
the compulsive emotional yearning. This objectified moment of relative
detachment may only last as long as you stay with it consciously. But as
soon as you go about your day, chances are you fall back into the complex (though hopefully to a lesser extent) and are less able to experience
yourself as a witness. The longer you work with a complex, the more
objectified and clarified it becomes, and you spend more and more time
outside the complex rather than inside the complex wanting what you
have always wanted. You can try using sheer will to move yourself out
of a complex, and there are times when this will work to some extent,
especially if it is part of a larger process. But the only way to transform
a complex is to wrestle with it *as it is*, to allow it to be and to speak,
and show you how *it* wants to transform. Such an attitude is difficult to
achieve because the detachment it requires is paradoxically developed
as you practice. But when Randy puts his dragon in the sandtray, he
has already achieved a certain level of detachment from hostility. He
wrestles with it there, and Randy and his dragon launch a full-blown
narrative of their mutual transformation process.

Jung again quotes Ruland regarding the living quality of the imagination and its ability to engage transformation:

> Ruland says, "Imagination is the star in man, the celestial
> or supercelestial body." This astounding definition throws a
> quite special light on the fantasy processes connected with
> the *opus*. We have to conceive of these processes not as the
> immaterial phantoms we readily take fantasy-pictures to be,
> but as something corporeal, a "subtle body," semi-spiritual in
> nature. In an age when there was as yet no empirical psychol-
> ogy such a concretization was bound to be made, because
> everything unconscious, once it was activated, was projected
> into matter—that is to say, it approached people from the
> outside. It was a hybrid phenomenon, as it were, half spiri-
> tual, half physical... The *imaginatio*, or the act of imagin-

ing, was thus a physical activity that could be fitted into the cycle of material changes, that brought these about and was brought about by them in turn. In this way the alchemist related himself not only to the unconscious but directly to the very substance which he hoped to transform through the power of imagination. The singular expression "astrum" (star) is a Paracelsan term, which in this context means something like "quintessence." Imagination is therefore a concentrated extract of the life forces, both physical and psychic. So the demand that the artifex must have a sound physical constitution is quite intelligible, since he works with and through his own quintessence and is himself the indispensable condition of his own experiment. But, just because of this intermingling of the physical and the psychic, it always remains an obscure point whether the ultimate transformations in the alchemical process are to be sought more in the material or more in the spiritual realm. Actually, however, the question is wrongly put: there was no "either-or" for that age, but there did exist an intermediate realm between mind and matter, i.e., a psychic realm of subtle bodies whose characteristic it is to manifest themselves in a mental as well as a material form. This is the only view that makes sense of alchemical ways of thought, which must otherwise appear nonsensical.[25]

As the "star in man," a "supercelestial body," imagination is linked to the cosmos. (Today we know for a fact that we are made of stardust; there is something in our material and psychological makeup that links our bodies and our imaginations to that of the cosmos.) Indeed according to Ruland the human imagination *is* of the cosmos and behaves like the cosmos in its pulsing, transformative, and creative properties. Imagination has a material presence in us. It is "a concentrated extract of life forces, both physical and psychic," and is of nature. Being of nature, it shows us nature: Imagination allows us to witness the interaction between psyche and matter. When you are in the imagination via *meditatio*, with a devoted attitude, you are in the inner workings of nature witnessing the shifting of mind and form in you. You are also in the soul of the world, the collective unconscious. In active imagina-

---

25 Jung, *Psychology and Alchemy*, CW 12, ¶ 394.

tion, you can experience the secret ability of the image to manifest and change, as a phenomenon in you that is also taking place on a cosmic level. You witness the miraculous interaction of energy and form in the image itself. You participate in the cosmic development of consciousness by interacting with that image. When you emerge, both you and the image are changed. A world has been created.

Today we no longer experience the unknown in matter as the alchemists did—we no longer experience sulfur or quicksilver as containing spiritual phenomena. But what Jung points out further down in his quote about Ruland is that we in our contemporary consciousness enter the realm of the unconscious when we look into the yet-unknown nature of matter or psyche:

> Obviously, the existence of this intermediate realm comes to a sudden stop the moment we try to investigate matter in and for itself, apart from all projection; and it remains non-existent so long as we believe we know anything conclusive about matter or the psyche. But the moment when physics touches on the "untrodden, untreadable regions," and when psychology has at the same time to admit that there are other forms of psychic life besides the acquisitions of personal consciousness—in other words, when psychology too touches on an impenetrable darkness—then the intermediate realm of subtle bodies comes to life again, and the physical and the psychic are once more blended in an indissoluble unity. We have come very near to this turning-point today.[26]

We have looked into the atomic microcosm of matter and found that it is not solid. It is not as discrete as we imagined. As Jung points out, the realization that matter is not solid brings us right back to the mystery of how psyche and matter intermingle. We know that our presence influences the way atoms behave, just as the alchemists knew that their presence influenced matter in their retorts. How or why we influence the behavior of atoms we do not know. We can only imagine what the atom contains and how it behaves; doing so, we see in the atom our own cosmic nature.

---

26 Jung, *Psychology and Alchemy*, CW 12, ¶ 394.

We also still experience the unknown connection between psyche and matter in everyday projection, where psyche and matter meet in a mysterious way. Projection is at least partly unconscious, by definition, and so contains something of a cosmic influence. It comes with the whole background of the personal and collective shadow. Projection, in other words, is a function of imagination; the psyche uses the imagination to project. Projection is a mystery and an autonomous process over which we have very little control—an illusion, to some extent, but also a psychic fact. Though we are not necessarily conscious of it, in projection we participate in the "realm of subtle bodies," the same mix of energy and form we experience in dreams and visions. In projection we experience our unknown or unconscious situation in the material existence of another person, animal, or situation. Even mechanical devices like automobiles can carry unrealized aspects of our personalities. We can feel how much energy a projection carries when it is tinged with love or hate. A certain strength of yearning in a projection can motivate us to do incredibly courageous or incredibly stupid things. That yearning energy and the voice that says to us, we "should" have what we want can be considered the combined spirit and soul, or the animating, mental essence of the projection. The projection itself lives in the intermediate realm of subtle bodies—somewhere between the concrete and imagined realities.

When the animating and yearning energy of the projection is separated from the object, we could say that in alchemical terms the spirit and soul are released not only from the subject that is projecting, but also from the object of the projection. When we realize something about a projection and work to withdraw it, the object of the projection no longer fascinates us—the material reality is no longer magnetic. A projection is a kind of mild, ongoing vision that is hooked onto a separate, material reality. As the projection is withdrawn, the person who carried it takes on a different appearance and dynamic; he or she is unveiled, and may or may not live up to (or be as low as) the projection. And, there is a corresponding shift in the subject. When a projection is being withdrawn, you feel different, and you feel differently. Who has changed? The subject or the object? The alchemist or the stone? You can really be impressed with the power of your own imagination when you realize how strongly a projection and/or identification has influenced you, especially when you were wrong. A full realization of the animating quality of a projection is an experience of the reality of the psyche. It is so powerful because, as the alchemists realized, projection is an experience of the same animating quality that lies behind all of creation. In projection, which confounds, inspires, and deceives us, the world soul is at work through us, sometimes goading us to wake up.

The alchemists could see the animating spirit rising out of the retort as a vapor, or moving like a salamander. They saw the spirit in matter as Mercurius coming forth out of the fire, or homunculi rising into the heavens, as we shall examine. Most profoundly, the alchemists experienced the animating quality of their own projection as the spirit and soul of God. Witnessing these images was thus a numinous experience. It can be numinous for us as well, when we realize how the psyche animates us from behind the scenes. Getting outside a projection is like peeling away the top layer of reality and peeking into the underlying dynamics of a less phenomenal world: the secret of the cosmic level of imagination. It is amazing, miraculous, that it can be done at all, because consciousness is so insistent that things are the way they appear. Randy insists on the validity of his hostility and can plainly see that others make him explode. But by putting his hostility into the sandtray retort and imagining what it wants to say, a gradual sacrifice of his way of seeing things takes place. Imagination is the star in him that helps him out of the projection by leading him through it.

Children live more fully in the intermediate realm of subtle bodies than adults do; their projections we feel more inclined to call *participation mystique* because they are so pervasive. Children really do see monsters in closets and lions under their beds. They are in constant *participation mystique* with the world. The alchemist's experience from our modern perspective is childlike. They really did see a spirit in quicksilver. But some alchemists were also sophisticated enough to know to some extent what was going on psychologically. They knew or at least had an inkling that their inner worlds were projected into their retorts. Somehow they knew that the "intermediate realm between mind and matter" was part mental imagination, part material reality. We cannot say that the alchemist's experience was "nothing but" a projection, because the transformation he saw in the retort was indeed a psychic reality. He was truly engaged with the reality of the archetypal realm—with the objective psyche. We too have to be careful not to dismiss our experience as "nothing but" projection if we are to learn about the dynamics and interplay of mind and matter—but especially if we are to learn what projection has to teach us about ourselves and the psyche of this world.

In play, which is in a large measure projection, psyche and matter, consciousness and the unconscious, meet in the third reality that binds them, the reality of the phenomenal world. They show us how the phenomenal world is real, and projected; in the third, combined reality the world can change. The child follows the inner impulse, and naturally works in that "psychic realm of subtle body" where transformation takes place. Randy stands at the sandtray with his hands in his own psychic material. "The act of imagining [is] thus a physical activity" that brings about material changes in Randy himself. The "stone" that is spiritualized as he works in the tray is his psychological situation, as it appears before him. It begins as a solid, unconscious and stubborn attitude, a hostility in Randy that has taken on a life of its own, and has its own, animating power. It is its own phenomenal world. In the sandtray this angry world is expressed, quite naturally, as war. When in his third session Randy says, "There is so much fire in these guys they just blow up," he points to an innate fire in him that has become explosive, a psychic fire that by its nature causes explosions in the material reality of his personality and in the world he sees before him. The explosive fire appears in the tray of its own accord, as both psyche and matter, and offers itself to be volatilized; this is the numinous principle behind psychic transformation. Whether in sandplay or in life, projection is the psyche's way of materializing before our eyes, in order to be experienced by consciousness as doing so. Once there is a retort like a sandtray, the fire in the psyche can burn *there* and transform *itself* rather than dismembering the personality. It is not only the body of the stone or the artifex that transforms, but also the arcane substance, the hostility itself, as we witness in Randy's work.

The alchemists imagined that their work on the *prima materia* could animate it, transform it, and redeem it from its dejected or unconscious state. The stone, like mythological figures who die and resurrect, can live again and again, a new, spiritualized reality in the retort, but also in the alchemist himself. We will see this "spiritualization" and rebirth of Randy's attitude as we move through his operations. His psyche brings changes about in the sandtray, and he is "brought about by them in turn." He changes, and his world changes.

The fact that in Randy's war of the dragon "one guy survived because there wasn't an explosion in him" tells me that within Randy there is enough ego strength, and enough feeling capacity, that Randy's basic sense of himself as an individual isn't obliterated. This "guy" is also "made into a real human," meaning he has the potential to be humanized, to be brought out of the inhuman and inhumane archetypal realm of war. The one who can be made into a real human is a transpersonal potential in Randy, an aspect of the Self that can be realized on earth, that is, in Randy's personality.

Chapter 3

THE DRAGON AS SULFUR, FIRE, AND WATER:
THE PHILOSOPHER'S STONE

The dragon is a profoundly paradoxical symbol, a form of nothing less than the arcane substance, the philosophical stone, or the spirit Mercurius. The following passage from the *Theatrum chemicum*, gives us a glimpse of the alchemists' awe for the dragon:

> I am the poison-dripping dragon, who is everywhere and can be cheaply had... My water and fire destroys and put together; from my body you may extract the green lion and the red. But if you do not have exact knowledge of me, you will destroy your five senses with my fire. From my snout there comes a spreading poison that has brought death to many. Therefore you should skillfully separate the course from the fine, if you do not wish to suffer utter poverty... I am the egg of nature, known only to the wise, who in piety and modesty bring forth from me the microcosm, which was prepared for mankind by Almighty God, but given only to the few, while the many long for it in vain, that they may do good to the poor with my treasure and not fasten their souls to the perishable gold. By the philosophers I am named Mercurius; my spouse is the [philosophic] gold; I am the old dragon, found everywhere on the globe of the earth, father and mother, young and old, very strong and very weak, death and resurrection, visible and invisible, hard and soft; I descend into the earth and ascend

to the heavens, I am the highest and the lowest, the lightest and the heaviest; often the order of nature is reversed in me, as regards colour, number, weight, and measure; I contain the light of nature; I am dark and light; I come forth from heaven and earth; I am known and yet do not exist at all; by virtue of the sun's rays all colours shine in me, and all metals. I am the carbuncle of the sun, the most noble purified earth, through which you may change copper, iron, tin, and lead into gold.[66]

The paradoxical nature of the alchemical work is expressed here in the allegory of the dragon, one version of the *prima materia,* poisonous on the one hand, and "the most noble purified earth" on the other. The intense feeling quality in this passage reveals that the experience of the upper and lower united in itself is numinous, an experience of the Self, or of God, as a *complexio oppositorum.* In the alchemists' devotion to the expression of this paradox we can recognize our own suffering of the opposites in the process of coming to terms with our poisonous shadows and realizing the meaning behind redemption. The highest and the lowest experiences of life come to us through our dynamic complexes, which drive us to our worst behavior, and yet to our most heroic accomplishments. The opposites exist in the fire that destroys and puts together, in the old dragon, "found everywhere on the globe of the earth." In the most common experience is also the most numinous. In every high and low is the Self, if we remember. Randy's dragon as such a paradoxical phenomenon hints at the fire that will emerge in his next sandtray and become a focal point of his healing process. The fire itself is engaged as *the* elemental substance that can transform. But if mistaken as being only common and not also holy, the fire more likely remains destructive in its nature: "But if you do not have exact knowledge of me, you will destroy your five senses with my fire."

The "poison-dripping dragon"[67] as the theriomorphic form of the common *prima materia* at the beginning of the alchemical *opus* carries the projection of the alchemists' unconscious, corrupt state, the dripping poison representing unconsciousness in its capacity to poison or degrade

---

66 Jung, *Alchemical Studies,* CW 13, ¶ 267.
67 Jung, *Alchemical Studies,* CW 13, ¶ 267.

an attitude towards life. In Randy that corrupt state is his hostility. But the dragon is capable of transformation, and represents the potential for psychic transformation in the alchemist. When engaged with the right attitude and with the grace of God, the poisonous dragon gives up the prized jewel, which is a renewal in the conscious attitude. Transformed from an unconscious to a conscious state, the dragon as a representative of the personality newly related to the Self, acquires a crown.

The renewed, purified, or transformed substance is sometimes represented as the *filius regius,* a king's son (and Randy's king will come forward in his session 12, Chapter 6). The symbolism of the royal or highest value indicates a new psychological state in which consciousness is related to its source and center, the greater Self. For Randy, this means he feels himself as real and valid; he feels his basic goodness, his royal right to exist. It is worth going into the paradoxical, strange circularity of this process, because every movement in individuation contains similar paradoxical qualities that are important for the therapist to recognize. Frequently we are confronted with fire and water in dream images, and their context can help us identify their meaning in the context of an overall process.

The paradoxical circularity of alchemical work—starting and ending with the same substance, which nevertheless has been transformed, is symbolized in the uroboric form of the dragon (Figure 5). Jung says:

> The dragon is probably the oldest pictorial symbol in alchemy of which we have documentary evidence. Time and again the alchemists reiterate that the *opus* proceeds from the one and leads back to the one, that it is a sort of circle like a dragon biting its own tail... For this reason the *opus* was often called *circulare* (circular) or else *rota* (the wheel)... Mercurius stands the beginning and end of the work: he is the *prima materia,* the *caput corvi,* the *nigredo*; as dragon, he devours himself and as dragon he dies, to rise again as the *lapis.*[68]

The circularity of the work refers to the fact that we begin and end with basically the same thing: the individual personality. In the begin-

---

68 Jung, *Psychology and Alchemy,* CW 12, ¶ 404, illustration p. 293.

ning that personality is one thing, in the end it is a different thing, and yet through the whole process it is the same thing, unique in itself. In the beginning the dragon is experienced as being black, because it is torturing the ego. At the end it is crowned, because it represents a new, noble state of consciousness, renewed in its relationship with the archetypal realm. Randy's renewal comes from his contact with the archetypal realm as engaged in sandplay.

Figure 5. Uroboric dragon with bat wings: image of the original *prima materia* out of which the crowned dragon emerges. The dragon consumes itself from the tail up, depicting consciousness assimilating unconscious material.

According to alchemical texts, the dragon is a form of sulfur, the active ingredient in fire. Jung discusses the symbolism of sulfur in detail

in *Mysterium Coniunctionis*.[69] Sulfur, because of its foul odor and volatility, is considered a chthonic being like the dragon, which is called
"our secret sulfur," the active quality in substances, the "spirit of the
metals"[70] which, with Mercurius, the spirit of nature, forms the lapis.
In this chthonic form the dragon is also the divine water, symbolized
by the uroboros.[71] So sulfur has its part in the circularity of alchemical
thinking: the sulfur is dragon, the dragon is the uroboros, and the uroboros is water. They are all the stone, and the stone is Mercurius, which
is the fire, and the fire is the dragon, the sulfur. This circularity brings
to the fore the paradoxical nature of the work, in which the opposites
are both polar and identical. There is duality but no duality at the same
time. The dragon may appear to be negative, as it does in Randy's tray—
"if you even touch the dragon you blow up"—but it is also a purifying
and creative agent (behind the births of Randy's bat fantasy, reported
in Chapter 9). The sulfur is a form of the animating essence of a drive,
and that essence has positive and negative qualities. Even hostility has
positive qualities, which is so difficult to see, especially in a child; as
a sulfuric influence, hostility has a healing aim and presents itself for
transformation. Randy's hostility cannot be ignored. But to really transform on an elemental level, it must be engaged in a way that allows that
opposite, healing aim to come forward. The mystery of the unconscious
is not only that it is unconscious, but that it moves into consciousness,
sometimes in the form of this destructive and even evil-smelling dragon,
sulfur, or fire, or water. Sulfur stinks, but it heals. Sulfur's volatility tells
us that we are in the *nigredo,* where the drive and emotion are gripping the body (see Chapter 8, "Sandplay and the Alchemical Stages").
But the sulfur's purifying ability also indicates that it contributes to the
whitening, purifying process that is an allegory for the purification of
the personality from its unconscious identification with a complex.

The dual nature of the fire is also in the water of the alchemical bath.
Jung points out in "Adam and Eve" that:

---

69   Jung, *Mysterium Coniunctionis*, CW 14, ¶ 134ff.
70   Jung, *Mysterium Coniunctionis*, CW 14, ¶ 142.
71   See in particular "The Visions of Zosimos," *Alchemical Studies,* CW 13.

The bath, submersion, baptism, and drowning are synonymous, and all are alchemical symbols for the unconscious state of the self, its embodiments, as it were—or, more precisely, for the unconscious process by which the self is "reborn" and enters into a state in which it can be experienced. This state is then described as the "filius regius." The "old dragon" who prepared the bath, a primeval creature dwelling in the caverns of the earth, is, psychologically, a personification of the instinctual psyche, generally symbolized by reptiles. It is as though the alchemists were trying to express the fact that the unconscious itself initiates the process of renewal.[72]

The appearance of Randy's dragon expresses the fact that the unconscious itself is initiating the process of transformation in Randy. The dragon, the sulfur, represent the drive in any complex that aims towards consciousness but may at first stubbornly exercise its paradoxical, opposite urge to remain unconscious. An emotional drive has a physical component that is conservative and a spiritual component that pushes for change, though the spiritual component may not be apparent at first. Driven-ness always comes through the body; Randy's violence comes forward in his physical bullying and cursing and seems to cling to him with great persistence. But when the dragon appears of its own accord in Randy's tray, the process of spiritualizing or volatilizing has begun.

At first the bath with the fire represents the unconscious state of the compulsion or complex—the original state of identification and wholeness: you don't realize you are unconscious, you only know you are in hot water. In a complex you are united with the unconscious, contaminated with the drive without realizing it. You might be identified with a power drive, for example, or a revenge drive, or a sexual drive that seems to work against your conscious will. You are in the water with the drive, but only vaguely aware of its effect on your life or on people around you. The appearance of a dragon-like image, or whatever form the complex takes in your own mythology, symbolizes the beginning of a process in which you begin to become more fully aware of your unconscious condition. The dragon making an appearance coincides with the urge

---

72 Jung, *Mysterium Coniunctionis*, CW 14, ¶ 548.

making an appearance in a form that you can recognize as something that requires your attention. When you realize you are in the bath with a complex, you have met the potential to move from an unconscious to a conscious experience of those waters. You realize you are in something that stinks, and that, ironically, is the beginning of a conscious experience of the Self.

Randy's wars for example at first express his raw, unconscious hostility. His first world wars express a condition in which the whole world, the whole psyche, is at war. Randy doesn't realize he has a problem with violence. When the dragon arrives, so has the possibility that Randy can experience the war as something he is in—something that envelops him. The dragon arrives with Randy's nascent awareness of himself. The dragon is the fiery emotional content that at first contains Randy in hostility. When that emotional content is in the tray, Randy can see it blowing people up. For Randy the fiery emotional intensity of the hostility itself is the same active element that brings him consciousness of his hostility. It really seems like an impossibility; it is a paradox to be sure. The emotion, the fire that drives the hostility, is the same drive that wants to become conscious. *Once it is contained in the sandtray*, the fiery emotion comes forward as the dragon to initiate a more conscious relationship with Randy. Although as a child he won't have an entirely conscious process of his transformation, Randy will have an experience of the Self in which the intensity, the essence of his emotionality, will become less gripping and destructive, and more available to him as creative energy. The emotional drive will turn from a dragon into a king.

It is helpful to remember that the *filius regius,* or the new conscious reality is, as Jung says above, actually a *state* in which the Self is or can be experienced. At first that experience can be negative—the dragon in its initial, unknown, common form can be driving us in a painful way. We don't develop consciousness in a stupor, but must be goaded. The dragon is the mysterious dynamism of the psyche that urges awareness, though sometimes through painful situations and foul, stinking neuroses. In fact, it can be merciless in the way it brings a stubborn state of consciousness to attention, or to its knees. In this sense the dragon or the sulfur is experienced as evil—as an addiction for example, or violence like Randy's, an emotional experience that literally tries like hell to bring

the ego into contact with the objective psyche and demands containment. An example of a seemingly evil phenomenon or being that aims
at consciousness is the snake in the garden of paradise who brings Adam
and Eve into contact with God's secret knowledge. The dragon and the
snake, both reptiles, have that "evil," unrelated, and cold-blooded quality that the ego experiences as negative. As archetypes they represent
the psyche's cold-blooded attempt to bring a new consciousness to the
fore. Randy's hostility is on one level a behavioral problem, but on a
deeper level it is the dragon-like emotional energy in his psyche trying
to get attention so it can bring him into contact with the Self. Randy is
identified with the hostility, and that can make him seem evil. But the
evil quality of his behavior is also drawing our attention to the fact that
Randy as an individual is buried somewhere inside the waters of hostility and needs to be separated from them. From a symbolic perspective,
and as the first indication of a movement towards renewal, the hostility
in the form of an ancient dragon is our guiding force.

We should consider the difference between the head and the tail of
the dragon in the transformation process (Figure 5). The head contains
the precious stone, or the image of God, which, as Jung says:

> means that consciousness [the head] contains the symbolic
> image of the self, and just as the lapis unites the opposites so
> the self assimilates contents of consciousness and the uncon-
> scious. This interpretation fully accords with the traditional
> significance of the dragon's head as a favourable omen.[73]

The possibility of uniting the opposites is in the head of the dragon,
in the conscious aspect, however small it may be in comparison to its
body. The head of the uroboric dragon assimilates the dynamism of the
body, in which the fiery urges and the unconscious hostility reside, most
unconsciously. Albertus Magnus describes how "the dragon devours
himself from the tail upwards until his whole body has been swallowed
into his head."[74] The dragon consuming its own body is an image of
consciousness integrating unconsciousness, the lower region of a com-

---

73 Jung, *Mysterium Coniunctionis*, CW 14, ¶ 141.
74 Jung, *Mysterium Coniunctionis*, CW 14, ¶ 140.

pulsion or attitude. We can imagine the dragon consuming its own body as the image of consciousness integrating the dynamic quality of a complex, bit by bit, until its sulfuric influence is no longer autonomous, or at least, not as autonomous as it once was. The lower region is unawareness, the head awareness, of a larger context, that is, the Self and the individuation process. The dragon is at the beginning and at the end, though in the end is crowned, indicating the realization of this larger context.

At the same time that the body is assimilated, the head, the consciousness, is changed; it is crowned. This can be a difficult principle to understand, because for us consciousness does not seem to be the problem. But consider how Randy's consciousness is stuck, identified with hostility. Sometimes consciousness itself is stubbornly enamored of its own way of being. The head consuming the body is consciousness integrating its own way of being stuck, or its way of being identified with itself. The ability of a conscious entity to integrate its own unconscious aspect is a paradox: the dragon eats itself. It must see its own innate duality, realize somehow its head from its tail, and then engage in assimilation. The hostile energy in other words must separate itself from its own urge to be hostile, and that requires the hostility to become conscious of itself. This happens for Randy as he burns: his consciousness is confronted with the chthonic, burning aspect of his hostility. Little by little the violence burns itself out, but this would not happen if consciousness too did not change as a result of contact with the fire. Because the active, fiery element of the violence is contained in the sandtray, Randy can experience the fire as burning itself out, and this experience helps the lower, chthonic dynamism of the fire, the gripping, concrete anger, go up in its own smoke—releasing Randy from the physical impulse to wage war. When the assimilation process is complete, when there is "no magic left" in the fire, Randy's consciousness to a greater extent is released from its identification with the dynamism.

Other alchemical images that represent the opposite poles of psychological dynamism are the winged and wingless dragons, the sun and the moon, or in Senior's *De chemia*, the winged and wingless birds. The winged and wingless dragons or birds symbolize the spirit-soul polarity that are united at first unconsciously, and later consciously, by means of the art.[75] Wings represent the ability to get above the gripping dynamism of a drive, or the ability to see, or realize the meaning of an urge. Or, on the negative side, wings can represent the way unconscious fantasy flies away with us, carrying us off the earth or out of life. Winglessness represents the earthly aspect of the dynamism. On the one hand winglessness can refer to the original lack of spiritual understanding in a dynamic drive, a compulsion. On the other hand a lack of wings or a bird with plucked feathers can indicate that the drive has been separated from flights of fancy; bodily compulsion and fantasy are no longer in cahoots. Images of the opposites engaging each other all point toward a potential shift from unconscious engagement in the dynamism of a drive and the fantasies it engenders, to the realization of that drive as a guiding principle in the larger context of the Self. Fantasy at this point becomes a higher, spiritual guiding factor because it is consciously engaging the unconscious and can help bring the urge into relationship with the whole psyche. As Theodor Abt says, "The goal of the work is the reunification or reconnection of these two aspects matter and psyche, or drive and drive-control, in order that these two sides of the individual can again work in harmony."[76]

Jung points out that the salamander, another reptilian, dragon-like figure that appears in the alchemical retort, is in fact the fire, just as the dragon is fire. Jung says of the this image:

---

75 Jung, *Mysterium Coniunctionis*, CW 14, ¶ 3.

76 For a wonderfully thorough explanation of the symbolism of winged and wingless birds and their relationship to urge, sulfur, and the sun and moon symbols in an image by Senior (Latin name for the Arab Muhammad ibn Umail) in his *De chemia*, see Marie-Louise von Franz's discussion in *Alchemy: An Introduction to the Symbolism and the Psychology*, p. 125. Jung refers to the same Senior image in *Psychology and Alchemy*, CW 12, ¶ 349, and provides the illustration on p. 249, in discussing the projection of psychic energy in alchemical visions. Theodor Abt's three-volume *Book of the Explanation of the Symbols Kitāb Hall ar-Rumūz by Muhammad Ibn Umail* continues and fulfills von Franz's commentary (presented in Vol. IA) of the late-discovered text by Senior/ibn Umail; the conception of "drive" and "drive control" in Abt's commentary, so helpful in understanding psychic urge and its relationship to the whole personality, is quoted here from Vol. 1B, p. 162.

The salamander symbolizes the fire of the alchemists. It is itself of the nature of fire, a fiery essence…It is an old tradition that, because they have proved their incorruptibility in the fire, such creatures enjoy a particularly long life. The salamander is also the "incombustible sulphur"—another name for the arcane substance from which the lapis or *filius* is produced. The fire for heating the artifex contains nothing more of the nature of the salamander, which is an immature, transitional form of the *filius*, that incorruptible being whose symbols indicate the self.[77]

As a transitional form of the *filius,* the salamander is present in the unconscious dynamism of a complex. But the reptilian form changes as the work moves forward, indicating a change in the fire-element itself. The salamander or the dragon at the end of the work acquires a crown as symbol of the new consciousness and its relationship to the living spirit. He is a relatively enlightened being, having endured the fire of his own nature. He has gone through the fire of unconsciousness and come out realizing where he has been. He has, in other words, seen and assimilated his tail. In a person suffering the fire of a complex as consciously as possible, a crowning moment arises when the complex is no longer all-consuming, but seen (finally, miraculously) in the context of meaning; its purpose in the process of the development of consciousness becomes more clear.

This state of realization is associated with color because it is at least in part a feeling experience. In fact, in the alchemical texts, sulfur is the element that makes color possible. In its positive aspect and a chemical that is still present at the end of the work, sulfur is considered the quality that "takes up color" and "shines like the rainbow."[78] The ability to take up color refers to the return of the color—the return of feeling—after the purifying, whitening influence of *albedo,* a result of enduring the fire. When the fiery dynamism of a complex has been fully worked, and when it is seen as having an aim and a meaning, consciousness takes on a new color, that is, it joins with a new feeling experience. The color also

---

77 Jung, *Alchemical Studies,* CW 13, ¶ 177.
78 Jung, *Mysterium Coniunctionis,* CW 14, ¶ 142.

points towards the *rubedo*. We will look closely at the color symbolism that comes up in Randy's session with the ancient-but-new wax, and how it corresponds with the emergence of the crowned king.

Ups and Downs

The circular aspect of the dragon symbolism has to do in part with the experience of emotion and emotionality. The dragon in the *Aurelia oculta* says, "I rise from the lowest to the highest. The nethermost power of the whole earth is united with the highest. I therefore am the One and the Many within me."[79] Jung says that from a psychological perspective the unity of lowest and highest within the dragon has to do with how the work of a slowly developing consciousness gradually unifies the highs and the lows of emotional experience. In an unconscious state, that is, when you are not related to the Self, the ups and downs of life take you with them. You are identified with what you want. You are thrown about by the tail of the dragon, the basic libido in the unconscious that appears at first in cravings or urges that you may not be able to control. But when you are related to the Self and can see your complexes from a perspective larger than the ego's, you are not so contained in the emotions. Rather your relationship to the transpersonal view can (gradually and for longer and longer periods) be a unifying agent for the ups and downs. You experience then more the head of the dragon than the tail of the dragon (God willing). You can achieve this state if you have experienced the dynamic emotional contents of the psyche as just that—you have faced the burning, chthonic sulfur consciously. "Purifying" a sulfuric, dynamic complex is not so much an elimination of an urge as it is clarification and containment. To contain sulfur, you have to apply sulfur, with devotion to the sulfur's own redeeming quality. That is, it takes practice, going face-to-face with the thing in yourself you least want to see. But doing so, the emotional fire begins to find a containing capacity. For example, suspend involvement and ask what is wanted; let the unconscious work on the unconscious by pointing towards the meaning of an urge. It is the sulfur that in Randy's *meditatio*

---

79   Jung, *Alchemical Studies*, CW 13, ¶ 267.

obliterates the characters that have so much fire in them: fire transforms fire, in the container of the sandtray. Emotional intensity wants its energy to be met in equal measure (channeled, contained) through creative activity that honors its unique meaning.

The various characters in Randy's tray ("135 good guys, just as many bad guys," etc.) are the multitude in Randy, the various emotional sparks, the multiple, chaotic reactions from the body of the dragon that is so mysteriously volatile, overwhelming, and dismembering the ego. The "one human" being who survives the war of the dragon, as we shall see, is the one who can contain and unify emotional content. As Jung says in "The Visions of Zosimos," "The genuineness or incorruptibility of the stone is proved by the torment of the fire and cannot be attained without it."[80] You can't get out of the fire without experiencing its dismembering effect, first unconsciously and then consciously. The lows and highs are inevitable, but they also lead to a new conscious awareness—a unity—and a relationship to the transpersonal depths from which the dragon hails.

By invoking the dragon and its fire, Randy enters immediately into a dangerous realm in which good and evil are not at a distance from each other, but so close together one may appear to be the other (e.g., the two sulfurs). He says, "There is so much fire in these guys they just blow up." Blowing up indicates a complete disintegration. And the way the "guys" blow up is tragic and dramatic. Randy holds nothing back as he dramatizes and completely engages the explosive nature of his work. He wants to see the guys dismembered; he forces them to suffer. His wishes seem demonic, and I really do feel sorry for the poor soldiers and animals that are so mercilessly killed. We seem to be witnessing a work of nature in which it is just a fact that some things must die by fire and there is no reason, and no mercy. And yet, there is "one guy" who survives and is "made human." Somehow in all the violence, one human being is redeemed, and that will be the jewel hard to attain, the new, less volatile attitude that develops in Randy, right out of the fire. The fire is threatening and shadowy, but it also brings about the potential in Randy, a new humanity.

---

80   Jung, *Alchemical Studies*, CW 13, ¶ 94.

The double nature of the dragon and fire is an aspect of Mercurius, specifically calling up his paradoxical tendencies as a threatening fire on the one hand and a redeeming fire on the other. (Fire purifies as it burns.) The poignancy of this double nature—the emotion that burns but also renews—can be felt in the alchemists' attribution of the fire to Mercurius as a numinous, godlike being who encompasses the opposites.

Chapter 4

CIVIL WAR: FIRE AND CONTAINMENT

In his fourth session, Randy conducts another war. A baby bear, who is "the monster for today," is blown up by a missile—a carrot—in his nose. When his father comes to see if he is all right, the father "gets a missile in the ass." Interestingly, a fire engine survives the battle because "its tank is filled with water" (Figure 6).

During a brief interlude in the action, Randy buries a gold star.

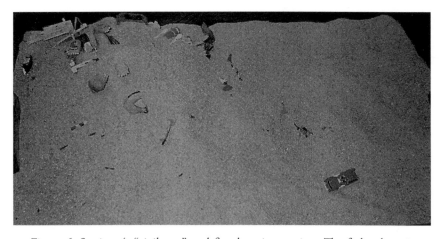

Figure 6. Session 4, "civil war" and first burning session. The father bear is upside down and buried in the upper left corner of the tray—again where most of the action is consolidated. A fire truck in the lower right may indicate the unconscious potential of water to contain fire. The gold star is buried in the upper right corner, which can be considered the quadrant of future consciousness.

At the end of the war Randy asks to light a candle. He wants to burn something. We are sitting in a tiny office, a closet really, in a public elementary school. I consult my conscience and my training and weigh them against the inherent dangers of burning a fire in an enclosed space. Randy is insistent, excited. Finally I offer to light a small piece of paper. As it burns, he watches intently and says, "This is the last of the civil war." He buries the ashes of the paper that burned, but there is more paper left. After four more attempts to burn the entire piece of paper, it is almost gone, ashes buried carefully after each burn. At the end he says, "there is just a teeny bit left." He wants it all to be burned and buried, so he works until everything is gone. When all the matches are used up and every bit of ash is buried he says, "they don't have any magic left!"

This was the first time a child asked me to burn something in a therapy session. I was nervous about it, but knew in my gut that Randy had to burn something. I have had two serious burning processes since Randy's, both boys. A burning situation requires intense vigilance and trust. When a child wants to burn something in the tray, I acknowledge out loud that it can be dangerous, and, if burning really seems to be necessary, I lay down a litany of rules (no burning outside the sandtray; water is at the ready; verbal cues are set to make sure we are both ready; know who will be lighting the match. The child must truly understand that burning cannot be done without an adult present; I do inform the parents so they can be on the watch). The urge to burn tells me that transformation is an urgent goal. There is nothing like fire to emphasize and illustrate the process of transformation, since anything burned changes immediately into something else. The redeeming quality of the fire, its potential to bring about a purified "something else," is present, but so is its destructive quality. Without the archetypal perspective, we are simply indulging a pyrotechnic urge.

Burning calls to attention the need for containment—containment of the physical fire, and containment of the corresponding psychic fire. The transference and counter-transference are intimately involved with this containment.[135] Together, client and therapist create the furnace,

---

135 Ruth Amman discusses the alchemical *vas* as a symbol for therapeutic containment and includes other parallels between sandplay and alchemy in *Healing and Transformation in Sandplay*, pp. 13-15.

the sacred enclosure, the *temenos,* that can contain physical and psychic fire (Figure 7). Jung discusses the nature of the alchemical furnace, also called the *vas*:

> Maria Prophetissa says that the whole secret lies in knowing about the Hermetic vessel. "Unum est vas" (the vessel is one) is emphasized again and again. It must be completely round, in imitation of the spherical cosmos, so that the influence of the stars may contribute to the success of the operation. It is a kind of matrix or uterus from which the *Filius philosophorum,* the miraculous stone, is to be born…One naturally thinks of this vessel as a sort of retort or flask; but one soon learns that this is an inadequate conception since the vessel is more a mystical idea, a true symbol like all the central ideas of alchemy. Thus we hear that the *vas* is the water or *aqua permanens,* which is non other than the Mercurius of the philosophers. But not only is it the water, it is also its opposite: fire.[136]

The *vas* is in one sense the container, and yet it is also the fire; it is even Mercurius, the spirit of the unconscious as it guides us in our work. The sandtray is for Randy the container of his fire, and so the sandtray itself carries the projection of the transforming substance—Mercurius as fire and Mercurius as transforming spirit. The container's spherical nature and its relationship to the cosmos is identical to an attitude that acknowledges the archetypal dimension of the work. Such an attitude exists in Randy as wonder, and in me, more consciously, as devotion to the transformational potential arising from the objective psyche and the containing influence of the therapeutic *vas*. I must be reasonably comfortable, and yet alert, to allow a burning process to unfold, to allow the fire itself and the devilish aspect of Mercurius, physically into the room. The intensity of danger on the one hand and profound healing potential on the other, makes the heart throb.

---

136   Jung, *Psychology and Alchemy,* CW 12, ¶ 338.

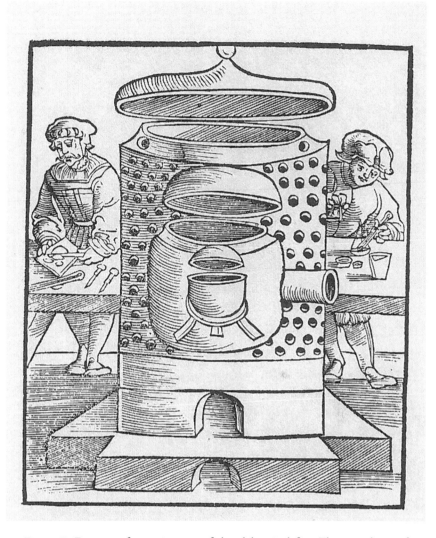

Figure 7. Furnace of containment of the alchemical fire. The roundness of
temenos in therapy is created by the understanding that the autonomous spirit
of the unconscious is present in the work. The *vas* holds the fire on physical
and psychological levels. The "hot" conversation between the conscious and
unconscious psyche, transference and counter-transference, is our collusion
in the sin—allowing the fire to burn, and to torture victims.

Awareness of the archetypal nature of the work extends to the transference and counter-transference. Randy and I contain the fire by virtue
of our relationship to each other and our mutual relationship to the fire
in his tray and in his imagination. Together we engage the intensity of

the situation— its danger—and we need protection from the underlying risks as well as a realization that something important can happen. We, together, are burning, and I must be comfortable enough with this process to participate fully, otherwise the transference will not be successful; the *vas* of the therapeutic situation will not be able to contain the operations that are pushing towards transformation. I must be as involved in the fire and nearly as awed by it as Randy. The fire with its engaging power takes us in—it dissolves the boundary between the tray and our psychic experiences. It also dissolves the boundary between us, intensifying the transference and counter-transference. In its transforming and dissolving capacity the fire symbolically is also the alchemical bath into which the Rosarium king and queen immerse themselves in the beginning of the work (Figure 8). The moment the burning begins, we are immersed in the sea, or the uterus, dissolved in mutual projection; the dissolving property is one of the things that fire and water have in common. Randy takes the work very seriously, and so do I.

Working with a child, I experience the transference and countertransference in part as a mutual engagement in the child's *participation mystique* with the activity in the sandtray. In the first place, I am experienced as the mother in the sense that I acknowledge the vital importance of the work in the tray as it informs natural development via the psyche. Through my acknowledgement, the child's psyche can enter sandplay as a transpersonal vessel for transformation. I must be completely willing to follow the child's lead, and to believe the way he believes, that the operation in the tray is real, and valuable. Yet the child's psyche is the "mother" of the fetal situation before us; the child always initiates the activity. We together are the mother. Our psyches together, or *the* psyche between us, contains us, because we are together, anticipating a dramatic event. The psyche presents us with the operations in the tray as realities—psychic realities. Randy's wars are real, and I believe them; I believe the psyche. Marie-Louise von Franz in the film, *Matter of Heart,* tells the story of meeting Jung for the first time. He described to her and her companions a patient who was living on the moon. Von Franz remarked that of course his patient wasn't *really* living on the moon, she only *imagined* she was living on the moon. But Jung "looked at me earnestly" and insisted, yes, his analysand was really living on the moon. Von Franz realized later that Jung was taking his patient's psychic situation seriously, as an objective reality.[137] Jung's taking that reality seriously was key to his patient's healing process. I must do the same for Randy: the wars he fights and the fires he burns are happening in the world, not "just" in the sandtray. His war of the ancient dragon is not "just" a projection.

When I take a child's work in the tray as a reality, I offer what I consider to be the working aspect of the transference: I participate in the reality that the unconscious presents to us. In this sense, we are one in the fire or in the bath. We are joined by psyche, and that psychic unity *is* the *vas*. Together we enter the heat, in which the unconscious sweats out its impurities. In *Psychology of the Transference,* Jung explains the immersion of the two bodies in the alchemical bath as illustrated in the *Rosarium philosophorum* (Figure 8):

> The immersion in the "sea" signifies the *solutio*—"dissolution" in the physical sense of the word and at the same time, according to Dorn, the solution of a problem. It is a return to the dark initial state, to the amniotic fluid of the gravid uterus. The alchemists frequently point out that their stone grows like a child in its mother's womb; they call the *vas hermeticum* the uterus and its contents the foetus. What is said of the *lapis* is also said of the water: "This stinking water [also called the green lion] contains everything it needs." It is sufficient unto itself, like the Uroboros, the tail-eater, which is said to beget, kill, and devour itself. *Aqua est, quae occidit et vivificat*—the water is that which kills and vivifies. It is the *aqua benedicta,* the lustral water, wherein the birth of the new being is prepared.[138]

Immersion in the unconscious situation is a dissolving *solutio*, but also offers a healing solution, as Jung says. The unconscious can help with unconsciousness if we engage it consciously. Within the bath is the water that can renew, but at first it is the stinking water, the amni-

---

137 *Matter of Heart*, directed by Mark Whitney. Jung discusses this patient in *Memories, Dreams, Reflections*, pp. 128-130.
138 C.G. Jung, *Practice of Psychotherapy,* CW 16, ¶ 454.

otic, initial enmeshment of conscious and unconscious contents that is also referred to as "killing," which means at first it engulfs a conscious perspective (an aspect of the *nigredo*). No other relationship brings this enmeshment to the fore like the transference, in which the whole mess of the neurosis and the whole hope of renewal are both contained, but at first unrecognizable from each other. Within the water of the transference is the autonomous germ that arises as a renewing possibility. In other words, the "solution" of amniotic water represents the unconscious joining of conscious and unconscious contents, but also the potential for those contents to be realized. They have to be separated to be realized, and so the bath has both aspects of solution: dissolving and purifying or separating.

Figure 8. Descent into the alchemical bath. The royal couple represents the masculine and feminine aspects of the original, unconscious condition; they are dissolved in each other and in the unconscious nature of the bath water. However, the water can have a purifying effect.

I hesitate to use the *Rosarium* picture of the royal couple's immersion because it does not seem quite appropriate nor even accurate when referring to a child and an adult: the two figures in the bath are in one sense the *anima* of a man and the *animus* of a woman, if we refer to an adult transference. As Jung points out, though, king and queen also stand for the body and the soul of the analysand, his consciousness and his unconscious. In this way I am not so hesitant to use the picture. Randy's "body," his ruling conscious attitude (king), is immersed in the bath with his current level of feeling for himself (queen). On the one hand the king and queen represent the original, unconscious situation—the way consciousness and emotional intensity are united in Randy's hostile condition. But their appearance as an image of that condition (or the appearance of any image of that condition, such as Randy's dragon) point to a new kind of containment, experienced in the transference, and the fact that a transformation is in the works. King and queen, spirit and soul, or we can say mind and body, psyche and matter, merge in the bath. The bath is the therapeutic situation, the *vas* in its archetypal dimension, the fantasy images in the sandtray and their symbolic meaning, Randy and his *anima*, and me and my *animus*. If there were no conscious awareness of the *temenos* linking us to the archetypal dimension, and the play was "only" play, the spirit and soul within Randy would not have an experience of each other any different from their existence in Randy's hostility. It takes an "other" for the container to be experienced, and this "other" for Randy is me in one sense, but it is also the symbolic dimension of his struggle, in which he experiences his otherness. Transformation in the vessel takes, as Jung explains, a "bond of love," which in our adult-child relationship is closer to mother and son than *anima* and *animus*.

> Thus the underlying idea of the psyche proves it to be a half bodily, half spiritual substance, an *anima media natura*, as the alchemists call it, an hermaphroditic being capable of uniting the opposites, but who is never complete in the individual unless related to another individual. The unrelated human being lacks wholeness, for he can achieve wholeness only through the soul, and the soul cannot exist without its other side, which is always found in a "You." Wholeness is a combination of I and you, and these show themselves to be parts of a transcendent unity whose nature can only be grasped

symbolically, as in the symbols of the *rotundum,* the rose, the wheel, or the *coniunctio Solis et Lunae.*[139]

Through two individuals, Mercurius is able to unite with him/herself, and hence unify his own opposite sides. It is the Mercurius in each of us seeking Mercurius in the other—the stone seeking the stone in order to complete itself. The autonomous power of projection becomes more clear when we realize our strong attraction or repulsion is the spirit of transformation itself seeking its other half. Mercurius is present in every stage of the *coniunctio* between conscious and unconscious contents; he is the spirit and the soul of that relationship, the yearning behind the projection and the yearning behind the urge to clarify projection.

The main healing principle in any therapeutic situation is this experience of otherness that occurs in the transference, whether between man and woman, man and man, woman and woman, or adult and child, which Jung describes as Mercurius seeking his other half. The transference from child to adult in particular is experienced by the child as safe, unjudged containment. If the transference is to serve as an archetypal, healing situation, the adult must be as open as the child to the symbolic level. Randy's fire seeks containment. It is better therefore to stop a process of burning than to engage in it without feeling confident in the promise of transformation. Otherwise, we indulge the urge in a regression that is not in service to development. If I have the attitude that we are engaged in "nothing but" child's play, I bring my client another experience of lack of containment. And in that case, the destructive nature of the sulfur is more certain to have its way. Randy experiences me as the "you" that is related to the archetypal dimension and a healing aim. We are united in the compulsion of the psychic experience of burning, but also in love of the *opus* and faith in its transformative power. We experience both the "lower" world of the bath, which is the compulsion to burn, and the "upper" world of the transformative, symbolic aspect of the fire (the two aspects of the stone).

We also experience the potential of relationship, relationship to each other but also to the Self (Mercurius seeking Mercurius), the healing aim of the stone. We are united in love for the potential in Randy, and

---

139 Jung, *Practice of Psychotherapy,* CW 16, ¶ 454.

for Randy himself, even as he is, in his wounded and hostile state. In my experience this love is not just human, but has the capacity of a deeper Eros. It is a weight off my shoulders to experience that my personal love is not the transformative factor in the transference, but that I am supported by what can only be described as the basic acceptance of a greater, unifying presence I experience as an aspect of the Self.

Another image for transformation—the alchemical pelican beakers (Figure 9)—informs our imaginations concerning the relationship between therapist and client, or between the client and his own imagination. The beakers pointedly illustrate the process of volatilization, or spiritualization, that is engaged so purposefully between Randy and his bullying. The fire in the bottom of each beaker causes a sublimation of the lower contents of the beakers (the physical fire), which feeds into the upper level of the other (the volatilized or spiritualized fire), and vice versa. Each time Randy engages the fire in the sandtray, an aspect or a portion of the lower experience of that fire, the urge, is sublimated into something more fine, and therefore can feed the higher, more conscious level of his personality (as with the head and tail of the uroboric dragon). If he were engaging the fire of his anger without a container, by acting it out on the playground for example, there would be little if any volatilization going on. Burning the fires in the tray allows him to experience the fire itself as "other," as something objective and yet inner, and therefore he can have a transformative relationship to that aspect of his nature. The illustration next to the beakers shows "twins"—another way to imagine the transformation of psychic energy when conscious and unconscious aspects of a complex are intimately engaged in a way that is mutually transformative.

Like all symbols, the water and fire of the bath have positive and negative qualities. The bath is "stinking" and yet the water of life. Our immersion into the work, and into the transference and countertransference, meets with the danger and the contaminating influences immediately, and we will witness great suffering as the dark aspect of Randy's journey comes forward. I acknowledge for myself the fact that destruction *and* resurrection are involved in burning. To allow the devil, destruction, and death to be present in the sandtray retort is also to be on the side of the potential new life trying to come out of that contained destruction and suffering. I set limits as a kind of prayer that things can go well, and to indicate to the unconscious that I am on the side of the child's individuality. I am allowing a child literally to play with fire, and

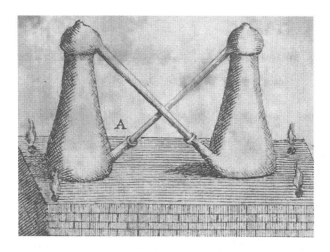

Figure 9. Alchemical pelican beakers—another way to view the transference relationship, or the relationship between Randy and his projected shadow. The fire in the belly of each beaker sends volatilized material into the upper level (the "head") of the other beaker, symbolizing the involvement of the unconscious in the transformation of consciousness.

this is very serious. At the same time I am allowing sulfur into the room, and this, too is very serious, because as the alchemists knew, sulfur has a devilish nature. Through the fire we enter the blackness of the hostile situation. But because Randy and I have each other, and because we are related via the Self, we also enter the fire as a spiritualizing influence.

Sulfur as Drive

Fire, like the dragon, contains the "secret sulfur" in alchemy. According to Paracelsus, "sulfur is everything that burns, and nothing catches fire save by reason of sulfur."[140] Sulfur, Jung explains, is:

> the active substance of the sun or in psychological language, the motivating factor in consciousness. On the one hand it

---

140   Jung, *Mysterium Coniunctionis,* CW 14, ¶ 134, ff 81.

is the will, which can best be regarded as a dynamism sub-
ordinated to consciousness, and on the other hand a compulsion, an involuntary motivation or impulse ranging from
mere interest to possession proper. The unconscious dynamism would correspond to sulfur, for compulsion is the great
mystery of human life. It is the thwarting of our conscious
will and of our reason by an inflammable element within us,
appearing now as a consuming fire and now as a life-giving
warmth.[141]

Sulfur is the chemical of drive energy—of curiosity, anger, desire,
growth, creativity, and ultimately, consciousness. When Randy says that
if you even touch the dragon, you blow up, he indicates that his experience of sulfur is more a compulsion than a life-giving warmth. It brings
about a disintegration of the personality; the explosions speak to his
tendency to break up into individual, emotional reactions. If you even
touch that "inflammable element within," it will change you. Randy
demonstrates that sulfuric fire is extremely contagious; if you even touch
it, you blow up. His experience of his own dynamism is explosive and
destructive. An explosion is autonomous and has a dismembering effect.
It happens of its own accord.

Each of us has had this dismembering experience in the face of strong
emotion. We do not choose our sulfur; our sulfur chooses us. The explosion corresponds to the suffering that can occur as a result of being
chosen to transform: its very tendency towards disintegration calls for
a more conscious unity. There will come a time when the spiritualizing property of the sulfur's dismembering power becomes evident, even
though at first its explosions are clearly destructive. Even now, Randy is
in some ways already engaging the positive side of fire, the "life-giving
warmth" that Jung refers to. In "Mercurius as Fire," Jung reveals how
the alchemists considered Mercurius to be a *coincidentia oppositorum*
because of his affiliation with fire.

> The mercurial fire is found in the "centre of the earth," or
> dragon's belly, in fluid form. Benedictus Figulus writes: "Visit
> the centre of the earth, there you will find the global fire."

---

141   Jung, *Mysterium Coniunctionis,* CW 14, ¶ 151.

Another treatise says that this fire is the "secret, infernal fire, the wonder of the world, the system of the higher powers in the lower." Mercurius, the revelatory light of nature, is also hellfire, which in some miraculous way is none other than a rearrangement of the heavenly, spiritual powers in the lower, chthonic world of matter, thought already in St. Paul's time to be ruled by the devil. Hell-fire, the true energic principle of evil, appears here as the manifest counterpart of the spiritual and the good, and as essentially identical with it in substance. After that, it can surely cause no offense when another treatise says that the mercurial fire is the "fire in which God himself burns in divine love."[142]

God and the devil are made of the same substance, according to this alchemical train of thought. Although Randy consciously engages mainly the hell-fire, he is also in contact with burning divine love. The love aspect of the fire can be experienced only in the *vas,* that is, in an attitude that can hold the tension of opposites—the fire's destruction and its potential to bring together. "If you even touch this guy, you blow up," Randy says. Although you have an emotional disintegration, with an awareness of the Self behind the picture, you also experience a creative potential as the secret aim of the disintegration. We will see this creative potential emerge out of the fire in Randy's later sessions. For now we examine how the creative element exists, ironically, in the destruction of the father and son.

Father and Son

The original, "old" state of consciousness that is contaminated by hostility and conflict, and its potential transformation into a new state of consciousness, are symbolized by the father and son. The son contained in the father is another image of individuality being dissolved. We are not at first aware of our consciousness being contained in an old or worn-out state, but we do become aware over time. In Randy's tray (still in session 4) the baby bear is the "monster for today," whose father dies of a "missile in the ass." The father and baby bear indicate the father-son

---

142   Jung, *Alchemical Studies,* CW 13, ¶ 257.

relationship as it stands objectively as well as subjectively in Randy. On the personal level, the explosive nature of that relationship is expressed

Figure 10. The king as *prima materia*, devouring his son. This illustration depicts how the current state of consciousness threatens to devour the new generation of consciousness.

in the tray as the baby and father die explosive deaths. On the archetypal level, the original father-son relationship represents the old generation or old personality as it contains the new generation of consciousness and attempts to keep it contained (Figure 10). Like the dragon, the bears in this tray—the theriomorphic form of the father and son in Randy's tray—symbolize the destructive nature of the original unconscious state. At the same time the bear represents the psyche's incredible transformational power as a force of nature. The psychological situation can just as easily stay the same as change; consciousness makes the difference.

Whether the personal parents are devouring or not, the parental archetype can have a devouring tendency. An experience of being stuck in an old way can show up in dreams and fantasies as the devouring aspect of a parent. Dreams or sandplay images of parents being killed symbolize the need to overcome an old state of consciousness. When we see how a real or projected experience of being held back by parents has become an inner phenomenon, and when we can kill that tendency, we sometimes experience an awareness of what Erich Neumann called the world parents, or the archetypal parents.[143] (There is another, more conscious experience of the world parents at the onset of adolescence and abstract thinking, and a child is suddenly aware of his existence in the context of the world, rather than just the family.) On an inner level, the Self can be a parent, as many have experienced through analysis. For a child in the therapeutic situation, the parenting influence that brings an experience of wholeness occurs in the *vas* and is the *vas* itself, the experience of the Self in and as the therapeutic container. Randy is not necessarily conscious of a re-parenting process taking place in him, but with his killing of the father and baby bear, he does express a release out of containment in its current state. As the old state of containment is destroyed, the renewed state can find room to come forward. A child whose life has been deeply effected by the explosive aspect of his parents, Randy is basically killing off the hostility of the parental experience as it exists in him, as the monster "today."

A father's concern for his dying son is rudely interrupted by "a missile in the ass," or we could say an explosion on the shadow side. The

---

143   Erich Neumann, *Origins and History of Consciousness*, p. 205. As Neumann says, the quality and character of ego emergence depends on the nature of parental connection, or the quality of what he calls the original unity experience. Although as an infant Randy's unity experience was good, it didn't last long, and the conflictual experience would have begun just as the ego was beginning to form and emerge from the parental container between ages two and three as its own "unity of experience." So for those years of ego emergence, Randy was exposed to deep-seated conflict and even used as a weapon, which would further identify him as a kind of explosive device.

shadow of the father is his hostility towards his own feeling life as well as the outer mother. The inner father for Randy is partly a "tradition" of hostility towards the feminine, or towards his own feeling for himself and for others. It is a tradition or habitual lack of relatedness in general, a one-sidedly masculine psychology of rationality and toughness that paradoxically prohibits masculine development beyond that of the warrior. Randy has been enclosed in this unconscious convention, the way the alchemical son or the new personality is enclosed in the father, or the old way. When the father is blown up in the sandtray, it is really this old, inherited way that is being blown up. In the next session the father is decapitated, indicating a further dismemberment of the worn out state of consciousness. In the same session, as we will observe in detail, the mother, the feminine value of relatedness, is rescued from the fire.

Lighting a piece of paper and burning it so thoroughly, and carefully burying its ash may seem at first to be a compulsive thing to do. But there is a transformative urge behind the sulfuric compulsion that is related to the birth of the new out of the old. The fire is a purifying agent and produces a purified body. Fire effectively releases the body from a certain state of containment. In this session the ash, which is a potential new attitude, purified of the old father-son state of containment, is buried—put back into the psychic ground for further incubation. Burying the ash is a clue that the redemptive goal of the work, while present, is not yet a possibility in consciousness, but for now remains under the surface. Randy's statement that "this is the end of the civil war" is a good indicator that the redemptive possibility will come forward because the civil-level of war has fought itself out. A civil war is a conflict taking place between opposing aspects of a single entity. Randy may be saying that the fiery war he has experienced as a battle with himself has burned itself out; the fire does not have its magic anymore. We can understand the burying process as an end, but only a potential one. You can work very hard with a compulsion, and keep it contained for a long time. Each time you keep it contained there is a kind of end product, an ash, or a building up of strength, and a concomitant loss of "magic" in the urge itself. What also gets built up as you work with the destructive urge is a kind of compassion towards yourself in your own war. When that compassion is present instead of self-deprecation for example, you feel a real shift from the red to the white sulfur—from the uncontainable urge to creative containment of the urge, as I will discuss further.

Star and Individuality

As heavenly bodies that shine like silver in the night sky, stars are related to the moon and the rhythm of her appearance. They are small suns, consciousness that shines, but only in the darkness. According to Jung's interpretation of the alchemist Dorn, the star-like sparks that appear during alchemical operations symbolize the light of God that shines in each person. Jung quotes Dorn as saying,

> He has implanted that light in us that we may see in its light the light of Him Who dwells in inaccessible light, and that we may excel His other creatures; in this wise we are made like unto Him, that He has given us a spark of His light.

And, Jung explains:

> The sparks have a clear psychological meaning for Dorn. He says: "thus little by little he will come to see with his mental eyes a number of sparks shining day by day and more and more and growing into such a great light that thereafter all things needful to him will be made known." This light is the *lumen naturae* which illuminates consciousness, and the *scintellae* are germinal luminosities shining forth from the darkness of the unconscious.[144]

Dorn identifies the inner light of consciousness as identical to *lumen naturae,* the light of nature that also shines in stars. This light separates human beings from other creatures, but *consciousness* of this light builds it up. When consciously engaged and accumulated sufficiently the *lumen naturae,* makes known "all things needful," that is, it illuminates the unknown in the human being, just as it illuminates the darkness of night. When we become conscious of this light within, our understanding is lit up by the light in the unconscious and its will. The *lumen naturae* thus

---

144 Jung, *The Structure and Dynamics of the Psyche,* CW 8, ¶ 389.

links the alchemist with the spirit of nature, and builds in the artifex an inner knowing that is related to the stars.

In *Ego and Archetype,* Edinger discusses the star as a symbol of the individuality that emerges as an *a priori* reality from the eternal Self. Having one's name written in the stars imbues life with meaning and purpose, "cosmic dimension and destiny." Edinger goes on to relate the dream of a modern woman:

> Following an important realization that she belonged to herself and not to her husband she dreamed: I was outside and saw a star fall... But it did not disappear. It pulsated a few times, then stayed bright and round. It was much closer than any other star—yellow-orange—like a sun but smaller than our sun. I thought to myself, "I've seen a new star born."[145]

Edinger explains that the dreamer's existence, reflected in the heavenly realm of the stars, helps her to see that her life has meaning beyond the personal realm, most specifically beyond her marriage. For Randy too, I believe the star could indicate potential relationship to a larger possibility. His reaching for a star is like reaching for an archetypal or cosmic parallel to his own existence, his own personal consciousness. The fact that Randy buries a gold star in the sand is a hint that there is a "cosmic" or archetypal goal, and an individuating influence behind the death of father and son that is yet under cover. The star as a symbol for the individual whose life is written in the cosmos, points to Randy's potential to develop an individuality that is more separate from his parental situation than is currently possible, and more related to his own, individual destiny. The star of an individual has its own integrity, which means though it lives among the stars of the collective, it shines by its own light and is relatively uncorrupted by the constellation in which it finds itself. The star burns with fire, indicating the positive aspect of the sulfur in its individuating capacity.

---

145   Edinger, *Ego and Archetype,* p. 159.

Chapter 5

NUCLEAR WAR

In Randy's fifth sandplay session, a nuclear war erupts. He sprays the sand with a spray-bottle to prepare it for "the big war." He uses glass jewels as nuclear bombs, killing both a mother and a father. Dad gets sucked into a tornado and loses his head. Mom is killed by a meteor. Randy says, "She is in the hospital, and they are trying to fix her back. At least her heart didn't blow up." I say, "You wouldn't want a mom with a blown-up heart." He answers, "You know it."

Figure 11. Session 5, a nuclear war in which the mother's heart survives. The water bottle Randy used to spray the sand before conducting his war is placed directly in the center of the tray. The water's ability to contain fire has a centering influence and becomes vital at the end of Randy's process.

Randy's wars are more intense, and louder than the average sandplay war. The outcomes are ambivalent. Good guys rarely show up; when they do, they are killed. His civil wars, world wars, and nuclear wars, indicating relative depths of psychic conflict, all exhibit the ambivalence and lack of moral ground we experience in archetypal forces. A nuclear war is a war at the core of the personality, in the Self. It is the war Randy was born into, a cruel aspect of his fate. But he has made it to this core now, and here something critical takes place; a heart is saved. The mother's heart is the kernel of feeling in Randy (and is reminiscent of the stone heart near the center of Randy's initial tray). The heart in this tray also seems to refer to the feeling capacity as the nucleus, the core that can be rescued. And indeed, the heart through the course of Randy's work becomes the central organ of his transformation.

The nucleus of a cell is its basis for future growth and development. It is the kernel, the beginning of its life. In biology the nucleus is "a complex, usually spherical, within a living cell, that contains the cell's hereditary material and controls its metabolism, growth, and reproduction."[177] In physics, the nucleus is the "positively charged central region of an atom, composed of protons and neutrons, and containing almost all of the mass of the atom." In chemistry, it is "a group of atoms chemically bound in a structure resistant to alteration in chemical reactions." In astrology the nucleus is "the brightest part of a nebula or galaxy," calling to mind the *lumen naturae* that shines from the dark. The word "nucleus" comes from the Latin word for "nut" or "kernel," relating it symbolically to the inner core of the human being. Besides all of this, Randy knows that the nuclear bomb contains what he calls the "fire of the sun," that is, symbolically, the fire of consciousness in its most potent intensity, its driven quality, its sulfur.

A nuclear war is a living conflict, within Randy's vital forces, his psychic potential, his core, and his hereditary material. It involves that which he inherited psychically, on an personal and earthly level, but also on the archetypal level. His heredity is in part his psychic fate, his karma; this war is his parents' and their parents.' He is also fighting the perceptions that have been developed in his teachers and others around him. Those perceptions, and projections of darkness onto Randy, have the potential to feed the hostile attitude, even to re-trench his inherited

---

177 *American Heritage Dictionary of the English Language.*

struggle. Physics tells us that the nucleus contains almost the whole mass of the atom. Likewise we know that psychologically the Self, its conscious and unconscious portions, make up the largest mass of the psyche. The ego is a representative of the Self, but it is the Self that actually makes up the largest mass of the personality because it contains past, present, and future potential. From chemistry we learn that the core is resistant to change. If we apply these facts to the psychic phenomenon of the nuclear Self, we realize it is not only larger and heavier than the ego but also does not necessarily want to change its makeup. The unconscious portion of the Self wants to stay unconscious just as much as it wants to become conscious. In Randy the anger, the fire, the conflict as a nuclear problem has both density and resistance to change. And yet this nuclear energy offers itself up to change "of its own accord" by appearing in the tray and relating to consciousness. I still experience this offering up as miraculous. There seems to be something in the "fire of the sun" that wants to be brought into contact with human consciousness, in spite of its tendency to drive the psyche unseen.

The Heart of the Mother

Although I would expect a nuclear war to be more intense than a civil war, this one lacks the energy of Randy's previous battles. The explosions are not as dramatic nor as prolonged. I am beginning to sense that something has fought itself out. Looking back, I see that Randy's identification with conflict had already begun to lose its hold on him, and so there is less energy in the war-play. His ego is less attached to the violence. It is possible that this nuclear war was the expression of a change that already occurred. Socially this change was evident in the fact that Randy had made a new friend at school. He asked me if this friend came to see me, and later began to ask if others came to see me. Discovering a friendship and becoming aware of the reality of others in his world meant that he was having a new experience of relatedness. I think this new (or rediscovered) feeling-sense is also indicated by the fact that the mother wounded in the war still has her heart intact; the center of the feminine is not blown up, but now can begin to function more fully as relatedness in Randy. The fact that he can ask if his friend comes to see me tells me that he is already beginning to realize himself as a person in relationship to others. In this sense, the world is a different place for Randy.

Spraying the sand with water is another clue that the war in Randy is losing intensity. He rather dramatically prepares the ground with water, which is the cold, moist substance that can balance the hot, dry fire. Water is feminine compared to fire, and can contain fire, put it out. Water is to fire as feeling is to emotion: it can contain the dynamism of emotion on an elemental level. When a compulsion with the intensity of Randy's hostility is worked for a long time through creative activity or active imagination, it starts to burn itself out as an unrelated drive. Such a drive becomes less and less of an emotionally charged obsession and more and more related to the ego, where it can be gradually experienced as a push for growth and individuation—an attempt on the part of the unconscious to relate to consciousness. If you give a dynamic drive a creative canal in which to flow, you begin to develop a feeling container for that drive. You become related to the meaning of the once obsessive energy, rather than flooded by its emotional charge. You begin to value the urge for its creative aim, rather than fear its destructive potential. To have a feeling realization of the meaning and value of the drive is to contain it like water contains fire. The water of the heart is also the blood, the redness of new life and potential that can come forward as a result of a creative engagement with the drive. We see this development occur further through water at the end of Randy's work. Finally, the alchemical water of life, the *aqua permanens,* is another word for the stone, for the liquid aspect of quicksilver. Without the feeling and containing quality of water, mercury would be only fiery spirit.

The heart with its feeling capacity is necessary to contain the meaning as well as the dynamics of a compulsion, and in this sense is the central organ of conscious development, as the alchemists knew. Paraphrasing Michael Maier, Jung describes how the heart is the sun in humans, related to the supreme consciousness of God:

> The sun, by its many millions of revolutions, spins the gold
> into the earth. Little by little the sun has imprinted its image
> on the earth, and that image is the gold. The sun is the image

of God, the heart is the sun's image in man, just as the gold
is the sun's image in the earth (also called *Deus terrenus),* and
God is known in the gold. The golden image of God is the
anima aurea, which, when breathed into common quicksilver, changes it into gold.[178]

The heart, considered in Maier's time to be the seat of the soul, is to
the human being as gold is to the earth. It is the highest value, the image
of God, in the human body. The fact that the heart here is compared
to gold, which is spun into the fabric of the earth by way of a natural
phenomenon, makes me think of the heart not as a discrete organ, but
distributed throughout the body, veined, as gold is veined in the earth,
and becoming more and more subtle as it finds its way to the outer
reaches of the body. God is known in this gold, which is also the soul,
the *anima aurea.* When "breathed onto common quicksilver," the heart-
felt soul of God changes the quicksilver to gold. The gold of the soul
in other words quickens the spirit. It brings the value, and the red-gold
color to the dynamic quicksilver. It is the heart, the feeling capacity, that
brings consciousness into the body, breathes into the body a new reality,
turning a common compulsion into something gold with meaning. I see
this as an image of God returning God to God, from an archetypal to
an earthly level, like Mercurius seeking Mercurius. The felt connection
between ego and archetype happens via the heart.[179]

As the sun, the heart is that in us which dies and resurrects. The heart
renews itself to engage in life on a daily basis. It is the organ that helps
us get on with our lives by valuing our lives in continuously new ways.
When we experience great disappointment, the heart in a way dies. But
the heart's connection to possibility gives us new hope and leads us to
new possibilities when the time is right. The heart is the organ that leads
us by feeling, sometimes consciously and sometimes unconsciously, to

---

178 Jung, *Psychology and Alchemy,* CW 12, ¶ 445.
179 In terms of the alchemical stages: There is in this image of turning quicksilver to gold an indication of a certain level of coloring, *rubedo.* Even a feeling realization of the archetypal level occurring in the beginning of the work,
a bit of relatedness between consciousness and the unconscious tinctures the
personality with the possibility of an ongoing union: the seed of the second
coniunctio is deposited.

our deepest lows and our highest highs. The heart is the clear-eyed witness of our daily foolishness. When we are too low or too high, the heart knows the truth and helps us by little hints to realize we are deflated or inflated. The heart is the organ that realizes and reflects our state of consciousness in daily life, if we can be open to it. Consciousness is an understanding in the head, but only can be fully lived or realized with the participation of the heart, where the image of God resides. For all these reasons, the heart is the gold of the human being, its core, and its highest value by way of nature. As the God in man, the heart is that which yearns for connection, and realizes new value.

A new feeling reality is the heart of the matter in any psychological development. The new feeling reality is just how we feel ourselves to be in ourselves, and in relationship to others, and especially in relationship to the archetypal realm. As the gold in us the heart is the main organ of transformation, via Eros. The heart takes the tincture for us and brings the new colors of compassion into life.[180] The gold of the heart as the alchemists refer to it, is related to the *lumen naturae*, the same light that shines in stars. When woven into the heart, that light lends itself to the personality as a guiding force that has taken on the tincture of compassion.

Randy discovers this highest value is not destroyed in his war. Especially important, the heart of the mother is saved. The heart of his original body, and at the same time the kernel of his potential new attitude, is saved. It is possible that by saving the heart of the mother in his tray, Randy's psyche has also saved and identified the positive aspect of the fire—the love aspect of the fire, as well as the realizing capacity of love. It is amazing, but a testament to the autonomous psychological process, that these life-giving, life-affirming qualities in the fire could be touched through Randy's destructive work with the fire. The nourishing aspect

---

180 During an early editing process I received Jung's *Red Book* and was touched to read in his musings about how to overcome the "spirit of the time," which the soul experiences as a deadly stalemate: "Scholarliness is not enough; there is a knowledge of the heart that gives deeper insight. The knowledge of the heart is in no book and is not to be found in the mouth of any teacher, but grows out of you like the green seed from the dark earth" (p. 233).

of the mother, the delicate center of Eros in Randy, is not blown up, and so protects against complete identification with the destructive aspect of fire and provides the core of the redeemed personality, as we shall see.

Chapter 6

COLLUSION IN THE SIN

After several more burning sessions, in his tenth session, Randy prepares for a war, again, by pouring glass jewels and stones into the sand. He creates a perfectly square paper box to burn, lights a candle, lets the wax drip into the sand, adds people to the wax and says, "Goodbye burning one. Goodbye friend." Those burning in the wax ask, "Why do I have to burn? It doesn't make sense." Randy answers firmly, "But you *have* to burn."

Randy adds to the melting wax a baby rabbit, eggs, sea shells, gold pieces, and a heart-shaped lock. One of these cries out, "Please God, kill the person who's doing this to me." Randy narrates, "It was Hades, Lord of the Dead. The Devil himself. But nobody can save them." He nearly adds a tiny pink baby to the mix, but then realizes that there is a force field that could protect the baby from being burned up.

At this point in the therapy, I had to address my own feelings about the burning process, which seemed to be going on and on. I wondered if the wars would ever end, and the burning seemed to become destructive. Is it overly indulgent to allow a child to continue in this vein, and further to let him use matches and fire? As the burning continues in this and future trays I wondered, am I helping him to turn into a pyromaniac? Is this really therapeutic anymore?

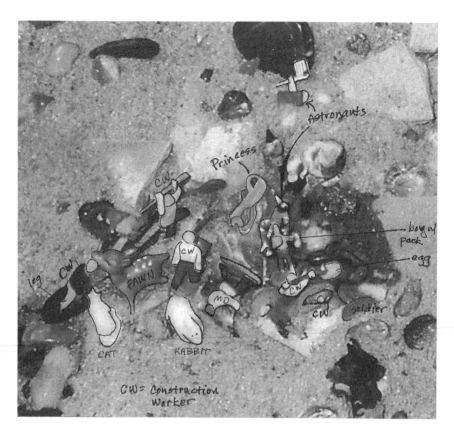

Figure 12. Session 11, in which Hades, Lord of the Dead, tortures people and animals through burning and melting. A force field protects a tiny baby from the conflagration.

The general rule in sandplay is not to interfere in the repetition. And yet, I must have in myself the conviction that the process is genuinely therapeutic. There is always the danger that the repetition can take on a life of its own and become part of the problem, and then the negative side has gone too far and taken over. I have learned to rely on my instincts to know when I should allow something to continue over and over, to "let it be," as Dora Kalff instructed. If I do intervene, it is with great caution, because the intervention can take us out of the *vas*. In Randy's case, the intensity of the imaginal situation is powerful, as is evident in his dialogue. Something in me had faith that I should continue on with him, witnessing and containing this detailed process. Years later

I re-read and understood in a new way this passage in Jung's *Psychology and Religion*, in which he discusses psychotherapy as a process of collusion in the secret healing potential of the neurotic condition (the destructive aspect of the fire) and the deep significance of the ego's drive as a "true will of God":

> Modern man...behaves as if his own individual life were god's special will which must be fulfilled at all costs. This is the source of his egoism, which is one of the most tangible evils of his neurotic state. But the person who tells him he is too egotistic has already lost his confidence, and rightly so, for that person has driven him still further into his neurosis.
>
> If I wish to effect a cure for my patients I am forced to acknowledge the deep significance of their egoism. I should be blind, indeed, if I did not recognize it as a true will of God. I must even help the patient to prevail in his egoism; if he succeeds in this, he estranges himself from other people... However wretched this state may be, it also stands him in good stead, for in this way alone can he get to know himself and learn what an invaluable treasure is the love of his fellow beings.
>
> When one has several times seen this development at work one can no longer deny that what was evil has turned to good, and what seemed good has kept alive the forces of evil. The arch demon of egoism leads us along the royal road to that ingathering which religious experience demands. What we observe here is a fundamental law of life—enantiodromia, or conversion into the opposite; and it is this that makes possible the reunion of the warring halves of the personality and thereby brings the civil war to an end.
>
> ...The psychotherapist who takes his work seriously must come to grips with... [the fact that rationality and religious faith don't always help a neurosis]. He must decide in every single case whether or not he is willing to stand by a human being with counsel and help upon what may be a daring misadventure. He must have no fixed ideas as to what is right, nor must he pretend to know what is right and what is

not—otherwise he takes something from the richness of the experience...[198]

If Randy were only subjected to rational and ethical demands that he stop bullying because it is bad or wrong, Jung's wisdom implies that we would lead him more deeply into the purely destructive aspect of his hostility. We would deny him his God-given right to indulge in his own hostility; we would cut off the projection before the projection could make itself known as part illusion, or to bring forward its healing power. The anger and longing would gain in strength were it treated rationally and conventionally as strictly an evil that should be stopped in its tracks. But if the "evil" tendency itself—the transgression—is treated as something deeply significant, then perhaps, it can lead to a healing *enantiodromia*.

Randy knows that bullying gets him into trouble, and getting into trouble fuels his anger more. I do not need to add to his guilt, only to his awareness, that the bullying isolates him ("Oh, no, you had to sit in the principal's office for hitting Billy? That must have been so boring"). I need to be on Randy's side. I need to be on the side of the anger and its potential to heal through its own fiery momentum, while at the same time helping Randy open the door to the remorse that is trying to connect with him. Because I am allowing him to burn, something in Randy knows I am on the dragon's side, the side of the "arch demon of egoism." The anger knows it, the unconscious knows it. And in that connection, I feel, the healing relationship exists. Our relationship is in the fire itself, and our secret collusion to let the fire burn is indeed a "daring misadventure." I know this instinctively, and yet I have to cling to this instinct when the burning begins in earnest. Especially when characters are subjected to torture, burned by "the Devil himself."

Torturing and Being Tortured

The vigilance of the rabbit, the life-potential in the bird's egg, the hard, protective shells from the sea, the heart that is a lock, or we could say a locked heart—all are sacrificed to the fire. They are told that they must

---

198   Jung, *Psychology and Religion*, CW 11, ¶¶ 524-530.

suffer their fate and burn. The motif of torture appears in alchemy as the suffering of the Primordial Man ("Psyche"), or Mercurius, the unrecognized spirit in matter, or the arcane substance that transforms.

The tormenting of the "substances" appears in several alchemical texts. In Sir George Ripley: "The unnatural [that is, evil] fire must torment the bodies, for it is the dragon violently burning, like the fire of hell."[199] The experience of the fire, or the drive, as evil, seems to be a necessary aspect of the transformation process at this level. I think this means that there is enough discord between the ego and the drive now that the ego begins to separate from the drive, and can more easily experience its devilish aspect—remorse is waiting in this ability to see the evil in the action. The drive is no longer ego-syntonic, and I would attribute this mainly to a development in the heart. With the heart of the mother saved in the nuclear war, Randy might be experiencing a new differentiation in feeling. That would account for his ego loosening its grip on the hostility, and the hostility losing its allure. Jung points out that the suffering of the bodies in the fire refers not only to the dragon in the retort, but also to the alchemist:

> A typical example of the projected torture is the vision of Zosimos. The *Turba* says: "Take the old black spirit and destroy and torture with it the bodies, until they are changed." Elsewhere a philosopher tells the assembled sages: "The tortured thing, when it is immersed in the body, changes it into an unalterable and indestructible nature." Mundus in Sermo XVIII says: "How many there be who search out these applications and [even] find some, but yet cannot endure the torments.
>
> These quotations show that the concept of torture is an ambiguous one. In the first case it is the bodies, the raw materials of the work, that are tormented; in the second case the tormented thing is without doubt the arcane substance,

---

199 Jung, *Alchemical Studies*, CW 13, ¶ 444. Theodor Abt pointed out that in the English version of this passage, "unnatural" is not a precise translation; in the Latin the fire here is referred to as evil, that is, in opposition to divine fire. (Personal communication with Dr. Abt.)

which is often called *res;* and in the third case it is the investigators themselves who cannot endure the torments.[200]

Jung in his text links the ambiguity of the torture to the fact that when something in the psyche suffers, the personality suffers with it, whether that suffering is realized as such or not. Put psychologically, the suffering of the "body" is the suffering of the personality in its original unconscious condition, stuck, unable to grow, unaware of the soul that is also lost, and in need of a new ruling attitude. Facing one's unconscious situation, one's shadowy material, causes torturous conditions in the conscious personality as well as in the stubborn aspect of the nuclear psyche that doesn't necessarily want the dynamics to change. Randy's hostility originally comes forward to be transformed by making itself a nuisance and causing Randy to be ostracized and lonely. Before he comes to therapy the torture has already begun. In Randy's tray we see the current aspects of the psychological state, as signified by the rabbit, eggs, heart-lock, and soldiers, subjected to fire or molten wax. The suffering of the investigator is Randy himself. The torture entails a detailed investigation of the painful transformation that is taking place as the burning is actively engaged. It is no small feat to transform a hostile attitude, and we are looking directly at the psychic agony that is endured in the transformation process—in the realm of the subtle bodies. What happens in the tray happens in Randy, mostly under the threshold of conscious awareness.

The suffering of the arcane substance is the suffering of the fire itself; the spirit must suffer in its own war with itself. Randy says, "It is Hades, the Devil himself" who is doing the torturing. Zosimos refers to the "old black spirit," which is tortured "with the bodies, until they are changed." The "old black spirit" seems to be the old black, contaminated way, the essential hostile condition that contains the personality. The "evil fire," in the form of the dragon as Ripley describes it, is "burning like the fire of hell." To be hostile is to be contained in a fire that burns like hell, but which is also completely convinced of its own validity and purpose—an aspect of the egoism that Jung described as a God-given right. Randy's fire, "Hades," is a paradoxical fire that on the one hand

---

200 Jung, *Alchemical Studies*, CW 13, ¶ 440.

is completely convinced of its validity and on the other hand causes its own suffering. The fire offers itself for transformation and from what I can tell is the essential component of the transformation of the "body." The alchemists say, "The tortured thing [the arcane substance], when it is immersed in the body, changes it into an unalterable and indestructible nature." This seems to mean that when the unconscious, hostile energy in the personality is tortured, volatilized, and becomes more conscious of itself, and when that transformed energy is "immersed" in the personality, the new more conscious and compassionate attitude can no longer be contaminated. The basic energy, the life force of the personality, has been transformed. If the arcane substance in Randy's hostile attitude is the tortured thing, its transformation through connection to consciousness produces an eternal change in Randy, and therefore in Randy's world. Randy's torture shifts from that of an ego suffering unconsciously in hostility, unable to fulfill his potential, to an ego that, having moved out of complete identification with hostility, actively examines the experience of suffering in hostility rather than relishing it. A subtle change of consciousness makes the indestructible difference. Something in Randy is far enough out of the hostility that he can look at its destructive effect. Though he can't articulate this experience verbally, he becomes conscious of himself and the hostility in a new way, and thus is separated from it.

In an adult this stage of the torture would probably involve some level of remorse, which is a torture of excruciating effectiveness. It is horrible to realize you have been identified with an emotion or an attitude, that you have been acting it out, that you have been inflated, that you have hurt others. Consciousness is tortured as conscience does its work—here we experience the close tie between consciousness and conscience. The relationship of the personality to the transpersonal dimension, gotten through the transformation process, is primary to its enduring quality. Once one realizes the transpersonal dimension of one's life in the transformation process, that relationship never goes away. An adult would have a clear experience of the Self as it guides development. Randy does not suffer remorse as consciously as an adult; he suffers it through his sandplay figures and the *enantiodromia* in the quality of the fire. At the end of the work, Randy's whole attitude and even the way he carries himself in his body changes. I don't think this could happen if the fire in him had not truly suffered an enduring metamorphoses, nor if the change had not engaged the transpersonal, archetypal dimension.

Finally, torture as Randy engages it, on a transpersonal level, expresses the suffering of unconscious contents (potential consciousness) longing for recognition. Randy's compassion, his feeling, his ability to relate to others, as we saw in the wounded heart of the mother, his feminine side in other words, is in deep need of recognition. This suffering feminine aspect is a personal as well as collective problem. In Gnostic mythology the separation of Christ and Sophia in the process of the material creation of the world produces great suffering on the feminine side because she is no longer evident in the world. But when Sophia enters the darkness of the unknown and suffers in the myth, Jung points out that "from these affects arose the entire created world."[201] In other words, the soul became invisible to consciousness as consciousness became conscious of itself and the world. The soul thus began longing for a reconnection with consciousness and a recognition of its divine aspect. Jung elaborates on how this myth expresses a collective *anima* problem:

> This strange creation myth is obviously "psychological": it describes, in the form of a cosmic projection, the separation of the feminine *anima* from a masculine and spiritually oriented consciousness that strives for the final and absolute victory of the spirit over the world of the senses, as was the case in the pagan philosophies of that epoch no less than in Gnosticism.
>
> The emotional state of Sophia sunk in unconsciousness… her formlessness, and the possibility of her getting lost in the darkness characterize very clearly the *anima* of a man who identifies himself absolutely with his reason and his spirituality. He is in danger of becoming dissociated from his *anima* and thus losing touch altogether with the compensating powers of the unconscious. In a case like this the unconscious usually responds with violent emotions, irritability, lack of control, arrogance, feelings of inferiority, moods, depressions, outbursts of rage, etc., coupled with lack of self-criticism

201 Jung, *Alchemical Studies*, CW 13, ¶ 452.

and the misjudgments, mistakes, and delusions which this entails.[202]

Randy is a young boy, and so the *anima* problem is not a mature problem in him, but he is dealing with a young, even primitive version of the neglected feminine, which he inherited from his parents' generation. He seems to have wholly absorbed a collective attitude that values power and rationality over feeling. The neglected *anima*, as Jung describes her, "is a creature without relationships, an autoerotic being whose one aim is to take total possession of the individual."[203] Randy's arrogance has that autoerotic quality that is so demeaning, prohibiting friendship or real masculine discernment. He is isolated by the "violent emotions, irritability, lack of control, arrogance, feelings of inferiority, moods, depressions, outbursts of rage, etc., coupled with lack of self-criticism" that Jung describes as symptoms of a dissociated, unrecognized *anima*. Such an attitude over time can develop into adult-level interpersonal violence, or a brutal rationality we see so often in men and women who cannot acknowledge their irrational sides. The mother's heart, however, symbolizes Randy's innate, undiscovered capacity for relatedness and in the nuclear battle, the heart is recovered and hopefully represents the core of a development in Randy that to some degree can be released from the torture of anonymity. The torture endured in his sandplay reflects in part the torture endured by Randy's natural feeling nature, lost in his violent and skeptical attitude and calling out to be recognized. It is easy to forget, when dealing with an arrogant and hostile attitude, that there is a soul in the background suffering unendurable pain.

One other aspect of the torture to consider is the suffering of the ego personality as it faces its own fate. I often had the sense that Randy was working with the painful facts of his life, with parents who were unconscious in just their own way, and whose hostility he was born to carry and now, transform. The terrible truth is that these tortures can come from the Self as just the facts of our lives, just the way things are, what von Franz calls the "just so" situation or as some would call karma, an

---

202 Jung, *Alchemical Studies*, CW 13, ¶ 454.
203 Jung, *Practice of Psychotherapy*, CW 16, ¶ 504.

inherited psychological situation. There is no other way for these facts to be dealt with than to suffer through them with the help of the Self.

A child doesn't necessarily have to endure the torture of the *nigredo* or the fire consciously for a change to take place in the personality. For an adult, an experience in the "retort" takes the form of a conversation with a destructive urge, through suspension of the urge and a conversation with dreams or in active imagination. The suspension of the urge creates the retort in which the urge is tortured. To suspend the urge and converse with it feels like torture because it precludes the usual release of energy through habitual pacification. Energy builds, and must be put back into the retort (one's own psychic-body). The containment of an urge, combined with a conversation with the unconscious about the urge, can produce the necessary "heat" for transformation. Active imagination can feel like you have locked yourself in a sweat box. Heat can also be produced through a creative process in which the unconscious is engaged. You can be tortured by the creative process if you are really trying to understand the meaning of something in your life, or your research, your analysands, the true meaning of dreams. The unconscious may comment on your creative work through dreams, and by that conversation, which sometimes tortures you by showing you your delusions, or sometimes introduces an idea you could not have produced yourself, consciousness is changed.

Rescue by Force Field

The protection of a baby by a force field occurs five sessions after the heart of the mother is recovered at the hospital. The "force field" is a symbol that we must go to *Star Wars* to understand, because that is Randy's association. According to *Star Wars* lore, the force can be with you or against you, depending on your attitude and the purity of your heart. The force is a guiding spirit for the hero, a power that is related to the gods. The force shows us the way, provides the wisdom to make the right choice in the right moment, as long as we remain aware of the force as an autonomous factor and don't become identified or inflated with its power. The force from *Star Wars* is closely related to the Tao. If the force is with you, you are in the Tao, and everything is as it should be. Conflict may reside in your heart, but it does not cloud your judgment or overcome you with emotion. The force allows you to discern what it is you are fighting—who or what is the real enemy—and to resist being consumed by neurotic thoughts, whether they come from inside or outside. I think of the force *field* as a protective spirit or an attitude that is in touch with the healing and renewing capacity of the Self.

In Randy's current sandplay drama, the force field protects a tiny baby. Saving the baby is a rare act of compassion on Randy's part, and may indicate that he is feeling the protective quality of the Self, and thus, his feeling nature can be engaged. In the fifth session it was the mother's heart that survived, and now it is a baby that survives. The baby symbolizes the new life potential in Randy, so Randy in a way is mother to this new life. His rescue of that life signifies a development of the mother's heart, of the feminine center of feeling, which Jung calls "the very essence of relationship."[204] The image of the baby is directly related to a differentiation of feeling, indicating the new psychological life that can be born from a new level of relatedness. As a guiding spirit, the force field protecting and valuing the new life is a concomitant development on the masculine side, an understanding spirit in closer contact with feeling. Together, the understanding of a discerning force, which is a masculine quality of strength in consciousness, and the feeling capacity of the mother's heart, which is a feminine, feeling quality, represent a mutual development that has produced or at least recognized the value of a new life, symbolized by the baby. This baby seems to portend the arrival of the king in Randy's twelfth session.

As a potential new consciousness that can be recognized, valued and saved, the baby in this tray is related mythologically to the divine child born into dangerous circumstances and needing protection. Like Moses, Christ, or the Irish Lugh, this baby's life must be saved from a threat that would destroy him and keep him from fulfilling his role as the new king or savior. In the mythology, the divine child is born to rule humanity with a new kind of compassion and a closer relationship to God. The birth of a divine child is often accompanied by a great longing in the collective for someone or something to bring new life, new

---

204 Jung, *Practice of Psychotherapy*, CW 16, ¶ 504.

meaning, to the world—to release humanity from its current torment. Christ promises compassion and love from God. Moses promises release from slavery. Lugh promises to eliminate the evil king, Balor. Humanity longs for these developments, and that longing is intensified by the peril of the divine child. Psychologically speaking, the divine child promises a new consciousness that moves humanity or an individual into a more vivid relationship with the inner center, the Self in its creative aspect. The danger it faces represents the natural pull of the unconscious to maintain the status quo. Although in Randy's tray a baby is rescued, indicating the possibility of new consciousness, its peril in the face of so much destruction is still very real. War, fire, and torture threaten to overwhelm the new development. There is a very real war between that which is trying to be born, and the old, stubborn, hostile consciousness. We hear a soldier begging for the agony to end: "Please, God, kill the person who's doing this to me." The Devil himself seems to make it impossible for anyone to be saved; and yet, the baby *is* saved. This means the destructive side (as experienced in the sandtray retort), though torturous, secretly colludes with the development of new consciousness. The hell of staying enclosed in the same old psychological attitude can gradually create enough discomfort to force the personality into a new possibility.

Longing as a Precursor to Consciousness

In many alchemical allegories, nascent consciousness is symbolized by a king who longs to be rescued from the watery depths (the unconscious). The new king, or the son of the king, the *filius regius,* Mercurius as the nature spirit, all are images of new development longing to be recognized, enduring the ordeal of anonymity. In his essay, "Paracelsus as a Spiritual Phenomenon." Jung quotes Maier on the languishing king:

> He lives and calls from the depths: Who shall deliver me from the waters and lead me to dry land? Even though this cry be heard of many, yet none takes it upon himself, moved by pity, to seek the king. For who, they say, will plunge into the waters? Who will imperil his life by taking away the peril of another? Only a few believe his lament, and think rather that

they hear the crashing and roaring of Scylla and Charybdis. Therefore they remain sitting indolently at home, and give no thought to the kingly treasure, nor to their own salvation.[205]

This quote reminds me not only of Randy's victims crying out to be saved, but also other analysands' dreams of figures calling out or displaying a certain longing, a hope to be heard. Something in the psyche, buried deep within the neurosis and isolation, is longing to be heard and is calling to the dreamer for recognition. To rescue an unconscious potential from the depths of the unconscious is the whole goal of sandplay and analytic work. Realizing the meaning of an unconscious potential renews the personality, and in the case of an adult must be done as consciously as possible. For example, a young woman suffering profound depression dreamt she was eating salt, absolutely longing for salt and was unable to get enough. The dreamer's longing seems connected to the voice that longs to be heard; the salt too is longing to be tasted. Salt is another aspect of sulfur in alchemy and can refer to the wisdom hidden but inherent in bitter experience or disappointment.[206] The dreamer could not "hear" or taste the salt in waking life; she couldn't yet fathom the healing potential of her depression. The dream in this case compensates the dreamer's skeptical and ambivalent attitude towards herself and her life potential and even her own dreams. Within her depression is the wisdom that wants to be tasted, but to have contact with that wisdom, the dream indicates she must really "taste" the reality of the dreams and their attempt to relate to her the deeper meaning of her depression.

Often a person or animal in a dream needing to be rescued has the quality of darkness to it, and you have the feeling you do not want to come near it. Or there might be a dream that brings a stink with it, or a pain, or a foreboding feeling. You would rather just ignore it. But very often the desperate or lowly figure or the bad feeling holds the key to real transformation if you are willing to go in and rescue the creature out of the unconscious—that is, if you can uncover its meaning. This is an heroic gesture that requires real humility. As Jung explains, recover-

---

205 Jung, *Alchemical Studies*, CW 13, ¶ 181.
206 See Jung's amplification of salt as a symbol for the arcane substance in *Mysterium Coniunctionis*, CW 14, ¶ 234ff.

ing the king calling from the sea means acknowledging your own dark
matter:

> In reality it [the king] is the secret transformative substance,
> which fell from the highest place into the darkest depths of
> matter where it awaits deliverance. But no one will plunge
> into these depths in order, by his own transformation in the
> darkness and by the torment of fire, to rescue his king. They
> cannot hear the voice of the king and think it is the chaotic
> roar of destruction. The sea (*mare nostrum*) of the alchemists
> is their own darkness, the unconscious. In this way, Epipha-
> nius correctly interpreted the "mire of the deep" (*limus pro-
> fundi*) as "matter born of the mind, smutty reflections and
> muddy thoughts of sin."[207]

Randy tells the characters burning in his sandtray that they must suffer, they must burn, that Hades himself tortures them. These burning
soldiers carry the projection of Randy's own darker aspects, his "smutty"
arrogance and hostility that is so far away from his relatedness. Randy
does not have to face these dark aspects in a fully conscious way, but as a
child he openly engages them in the arena of play as energies in the warring attitude. In this way they have an effect on Randy's consciousness,
and vice versa. His consciousness tells his own warring energies they
must remain in pain and suffer their fate until their time is up. As fighting aspects the soldiers are subjected to torment until the torment does
its job and the fighters are transformed. If and when this happens, we
could say that the "arch demon of egoism" has helped lead to a possible
enantiodromia in which Randy helps rescue his more related potential.

---

207 Jung, *Alchemical Studies*, CW 13, ¶ 183.

Chapter 7

KING OF THE BLOODFIRE

In Randy's twelfth session he lights a red candle contained in a glass jar. As the fire burns, he pours the melted wax into the sand and calls the molten fluid "a river of blood," mesmerized by the way it moves and flows. He holds his hands over the smoke and blackens them. Smudging his arms and face with the soot, he declares himself "king of the blood-fire" (Figures 13 and 14) .

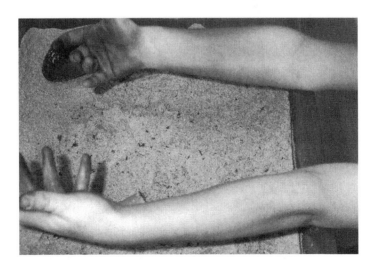

Figure 13. Session 12. Randy declares himself "king of the bloodfire" and smears himself with ash. Ash is a form of the alchemical *prima materia*, referred to in the *Chymical wedding* as the "diadem of thy heart."

No one is burned today. Randy burns small pieces of paper. He is quiet.

Playing with the melted wax, he suddenly he cries out, "Men, Men! I've discovered wax from ancient times! We are the haves! For once, we are the haves! We've discovered something new, finally, finally! Its entirely completely new! But we don't know what it is!" He sings: "We've discovered something new in the world."

He brings to the tray "Princess Aurora" and says to her, "Majesty, it's part of your collection. I remember it being black, not pink. But it was pink, not black!"

Digging with his fingers, he pulls all of the warm wax out of the jar. He forms the wax into a red ball. He sets the ball of wax and the emptied jar next to each other in the center of the tray (Figure 14). He declares, "That wasn't a million years ago! It was three years ago!"

Figure 14. Also in Session 12, Randy melts a red candle, watching the wax burn and run through the sand. He pulls all the wax out of the container and announces he has found an ancient wax that has never been seen before. He says the wax is part of Princess Aurora's "collection."

Randy's declaration that he has found "wax from ancient times" that is also "entirely, completely new" beautifully expresses the paradox of the alchemical king who was old and suffered under the sea, but is finally discovered as a new entity that can rule. When the alchemist finally hears the call of the old king and goes into the darkness and the fire to rescue him, that is when the new king, the new consciousness, can begin to emerge:

> The alchemists [saw that] the dark background of the soul contains not only evil but a king in need of, and capable of, redemption, of whom the Rosarium says, "at the end of the work the king will go forth for thee, crowned with his diadem, radiant as the sun, shining like the carbuncle, constant in the fire..."[223]

The dark background of Randy's wars has contained the destructive quality of his violent, fighting drive. But languishing in the darkness was also the "king of the bloodfire," who emerges after the baby is rescued from the fire, and before that, the heart of the mother is saved. In the symbol of the king we again find the paradoxical circularity that we encountered with the dragon, for the king is another form of the dragon, and both are the stone that transforms. First, the king is the old king—the original psychic situation, calling out from the "dark background of the soul" for attention. Second, the king is the fire itself. He transforms as fire and retains its constancy. Third, he emerges from the fire as the new king. The new king is the *filius regius,* the son of the old king, just as the baby that Randy rescues is in a sense his own son, his new psychological and spiritual possibility. And finally the new king is the enduring product of the fire, the ash, referred to in the *Chymical Wedding* as the crown of the heart:

> And of the worthless *prima materia* they say, "despise not the ashes, for they are thy diadem of the heart, and the ash of things that endure."[224]

---

223 Jung, *Alchemical Studies*, CW 13, ¶ 183.
224 Jung, *Mysterium Coniunctionis*, CW 14, ¶ 247.

Ash as a by-product of the fire is considered a crowning substance. Ash crowns the heart, and endures. The purified by-product of intense suffering and torture, the ash represents the new psychic substance, the consciousness that is in and of the heart. It lives in the heart as an enduring feeling capacity. The new king is the new ruling principle in consciousness, but as we know from mythology and fairy tales, the new king rarely comes to rule without also having a new queen by his side, and vice versa. According to this alchemical quote and according to Randy's previous trays, the heart is the center, and perhaps the fixative, of the new ruling principle of consciousness. The heart is the site of new realization; when it is crowned, its ability to realize a new truth is recognized as the highest value. It is ultimately the heart that is transformed in the fire, and the ash, the evidence of that heart-transformation, is the crowning achievement of the new development.

The new king is a symbol of a renewal in the Self, achieved in part through the suffering of the old conscious attitude, and in part the potential that suffered unrecognized in the unconscious. When Randy declares himself king of the bloodfire, he makes it known that he is in contact with the new king. He is declaring that he rules the passion, at least more than he did in the past; the passion does not rule him, doesn't blow him apart anymore. Smearing himself with the ash as he makes this declaration, he identifies with the enduring, transformed substance, his true nature, lost in hostility, that has been through a grueling transmutation. It makes the hairs on my neck stand on end to think of the actual ash in Randy's tray as the material manifestation of a new psychic reality with which Randy can now be joined. The ash carries the projection of his new royal consciousness, but it also seems to exist for Randy as the psychic substance produced by the long purification process inherent in his burning. This is one of those situations when the phenomenon "projection" may not adequately describe the reality of the subtle realm being experienced. Randy's urge to smear himself with the ash indicates that the ash itself carries a magical quality, mana, through which Randy can experience himself as a new kind of reality, a king with a heart. He (Randy's ego) of course is not the king; the new psychic reality *in* Randy is the king. But Randy is now in union with that reality as the ash; his ego has discovered something brand new to identify with, and that quality, that ash, the crowning achievement of the heart, is the feeling capacity that can value and realize a new kind of strength.

A New Ball of Wax

Randy further demonstrates the material-yet-spiritual quality of his discovery when he makes a ball of wax out of the candle he had been burning as if to say, there is now a "new ball of wax" in the tray, corresponding to a new psychic reality. The candle isn't the candle anymore, which was used to melt soldiers. It is a new reality, a new "body," identical to a newly formed ego-consciousness, produced out of the burning and related to a renewal in the Self. Though crude, it is a mandala, signifying the ego-Self relationship. As a newly discovered reality, the ball of wax is an example of the world-producing function of the ego-Self engagement. As the Self is renewed through an active conscious engagement, the world changes. The new wax is a physical reality to Randy, imbued with numinous meaning. His imagination projects onto the wax an inner reality that has been melted down, mortified, and re-solidified in the psyche. It is ancient yet new. The new aspect is partly unconscious, projected into the wax, but partly conscious, in Randy's experience of himself as a new reality—a friend, a good student, a valuable, basically good, individual. Jung describes the alchemical experience of such a new psychological reality, partly conscious and partly unconscious:

> The soul, says our author [Sendivogius], is only partly confined to the body, just as God is only partly enclosed in the body of the world. If we strip this statement of its metaphysics it asserts that the psyche is only partly identical with our empirical conscious being; for the rest it is projected and in this state it imagines or realizes those greater things which the body cannot grasp, i.e., cannot bring into reality.[225]

The discovery of an ancient wax that is also completely new is a profound example of "greater things which the body cannot grasp," a psychic reality that could not have been imagined by Randy's previous

---

225 Jung, *Psychology and Alchemy*, CW 12, ¶ 399. Sendivogius is the author of "De sulphure," *Musaeum hermeticum*, beginning on p. 601.

level of development. The ego's new realization reflects a corresponding development in the Self, which remains to some extent unconscious and therefore, for Randy, projected into the wax. Even though the ego cannot grasp nor describe what has happened in every aspect, the ego does experience an awakening, a realization, a new reality. The wax represents a new possibility in Randy, and yet its manifestation remains mysterious. Being from ancient times, it seems to emerge from the collective unconscious.

The red ball of wax symbolizes the new red sun that rises in the East. Randy says it was black but now it is pink. It has been through the dark journey of the underworld and now appears as a new phenomenon, a resurrected reality. It was a black fire but is now a red fire, an indication of a new, living consciousness instead of an old, evil fire. In Egypt the rising sun is said to be red with Hathor's blood, who gives birth to it.[226] The red sun is associated psychologically with the birth of something new and is not the same as the yellow sun, which symbolizes the yellow-gold of an achieved, steady, daylight consciousness. The red wax as a new sun is still a possibility, not quite reaching fully into consciousness as a steady reality. It is numinous because it is new and holds so much potential in the personality.

Now Randy says, the discovery took place only "three years ago," not three million years ago, which brings the wax into the personal realm. Three years ago Randy was three, and his parents were separating, beginning Randy's experience in and as a hostile reality. The new discovery is the old thing, either three million or three years old, or both. This is exactly how it happens when an unconscious content is made conscious. We experience the brand new discovery of an old thing, an old energy, sometimes one that goes back through the generations, God knows how far. To the extent that we can integrate such ancient material, we give something back to history and to the collective. We achieve a new level of personal freedom from the very old, dominating attitude, and in the process discover the genuine individuality that also was always there.

Randy notes the wax as being part of Princess Aurora's "collection." The collection that he works with is my collection of miniatures, so in

---

226 Thanks to Theodor Abt for this association.

one sense he is saying that the new ball of wax is part of my collection or my psyche. I could feel in that moment the strength of the transference and counter-transference phenomenon, and that this new red sun, this development, was taking place by virtue of the transference. In one sense the new development is part of my collection of psychological realities, because I have helped bring it to birth. But this new sun really belongs to Randy, and our work in later sessions helps him claim the new development more empirically as his own. Eventually his development is fully integrated into his life; such an integration is an aspect of the *rubedo* stage of his work (fully explored in Chapter 8).

Saying that the ball of wax is part of Princess Aurora's collection, Randy also seems to be indicating that the new reality in him belongs to the feminine side. Randy is very familiar with the Star Wars characters. The figure he chose is actually Padmé Amidala wearing a red robe, so it is important that he calls her by a different name.

Aurora is the light of dawn, or the light of new consciousness, associated with the rising sun, just as the red ball of wax is related to the rising sun. Making the new "body" of wax a part of Aurora's collection indicates that whatever realization he may or may not have about his new consciousness, he is experiencing it on the feminine side. The new reality he has discovered is related to the feminine, the suffering soul or *anima*, the compassion, once lost in the darkness of his hostility. Princess Aurora may be a new development that arose from the heart of the mother once threatened in the heat of battle, and in so much danger. The heart was rescued, and now perhaps it has a new life, a new, animated feeling reality, something like the quiet thrill of dawn we feel when we discover a new compassion in ourselves. Randy's new experience of compassion for himself (feminine feeling) frees him now to achieve new goals (masculine action).

Chapter 8

SANDPLAY AND THE ALCHEMICAL STAGES

I have hinted at the alchemical stages of Randy's work and would like to bring those stages more fully into view, as they relate to sandplay. Summarizing Randy's process so far: Randy's bullying attitude has come forward in the retort of the sandtray as war and fire. Over several burning sessions, the fire has produced an ash that Randy recognizes as important enough to smear on himself. The fire also produced "ancient wax," that is paradoxically brand new, that is, discovered for the first time in Randy's psychological history. Out of this ash and wax emerges the "king of the bloodfire," indicating at least in potential a new ruling attitude, one that is becoming immune to the fiery violence that has been blazing away in the safe container of the sandtray. Gradually as this process has developed, Randy's psychological situation has changed, and he has begun to make friends and adapt to school. In alchemical terms, Randy shows signs of moving from the *nigredo* stage of black confusion to the *albedo* stage of white purity, and there are indications that he can move towards the third, *rubedo* stage in which the white condition becomes "reddened" with new life. These stages are never quite discrete in any sandplay or analytic process. They overlap with each other. But they do bear clear signals that they are active, and we can see these signals expressed in Randy's work. I want to emphasize that the alchemical stages *cannot be prescribed*. These stages of the alchemical *opus* were not "created" by an alchemist on a conceptual or philosophical level. Rather, the stages were discovered; they indicate archetypal phenomena that arise spontaneously from the unconscious when the autonomous psyche is seriously engaged in a healing process. They indicate general patterns in psychic transformation that seem to be as true today as they were in ancient alchemy, although the content of transformation is eternally varied and depends on the individual. The alchemical *opus* is never really finished, reflecting the fact that individuation is never really finished, enlightenment not a permanent state. We go through cycles of change in our lives, some more pronounced than others, some with ongoing themes.

A *nigredo* state in a person's psychology we can generally say refers to an unconscious identification with an old, worn-out attitude. It is often expressed in a neurotic condition, which indicates that in the unconscious too, there is a calling out for renewal. The Self is constantly renewing itself, and needs the ego to recognize that need. Randy has been identified with hostility that has made his life hell for himself and others. At first his hostility may have been protective, a way to survive, but now it no longer serves him and is worn out, reflecting a need for renewal. Hostility contaminates his personality. Others may be identified with depression, anxiety, power, their own intelligence, body image, etc. Such an identification can happen to anyone at any time, since at any time we can become blind to our own attitudes. Some attitudes take a lifetime to move through. Some never transform. Unconscious identification is incredibly powerful, because it is, after all, unconscious. Consciousness can see its unconscious identification in dreams and active imagination, and sometimes in projection if caught *en flagrante*.[223] As a form of active imagination, sandplay allows the black, destructive, suffocating, unconscious situation to come forward and be engaged in the retort of the sandtray.

An alchemical analogy for a personality in an unconscious, *nigredo* state, is the *massa confusa,* a mass, or lump, of confusion. Randy's personality, which we can think of as the original mass, is contaminated, without self-reflection, by violence and ambivalence. To get to the purified "stone," the personality or mass freed of its unconscious identifi-

---

223 'In the act' or 'red handed.'

cation with a complex, the impurity itself, the contaminated attitude, goes into the sandtray retort where it can be worked. Projected into the retort, the unconscious situation is burned, boiled, melted down, flooded, washed, decapitated, dismembered, and left for dead—all aspects of the work that come forward in the *nigredo* stage as operations through which the unconscious condition may release itself. In analytic work this dismantling is equally as detailed, even tediously so, as each grain of the unconscious condition is examined and analyzed ("purified" of unconsciousness). Of course, the alchemists generally did not realize they were working with their own psychic states in their retorts; they saw themselves as extracting a purified, spiritual essence out of a common, evil, or impure lump of matter. It was Jung who realized that in their *opus*, the alchemists experienced the yearning of their own souls for contact with consciousness.

The state of "confusion," in which a worn out condition contaminates the ego with an attitude that prevents development, frequently appears in sandtrays as literal chaos. Randy's initial tray (Figure 2) was strewn with the remnants of an intense bombing campaign. We see animals, buildings, trucks, stones, and jewels scattered and destroyed without an obvious sense of structure or organization. Dora Kalff recognized such images in sandplay as expressing an unhealthy, weak, or unconsciously destructive formation of the ego-structure.[224] Such a problem reflects a need for renewal on the level of the Self, and requires the unconscious to participate in the healing process. She recognized how crucial it is that the initial state of chaos be expressed, first of all, and that it be contained in the safe and sheltered space provided by sandplay therapy. A therapist is very careful not to criticize, suggest, or be overly awed by initial chaos, because we want it to come forward without shame or self-consciousness. This is why, when Randy in his initial session dumps a bowlful of glass jewels into the tray, clearly wondering if he is sparking a reaction from me, I say only, "That's a lot of bombs!" I want to react in a way that encourages the unconscious situation to present itself as fully as possible. Once the chaos of the situation is expressed in the sandtray, it can lend itself to an ongoing process of organization and purification. Randy doesn't know he is identified with violence, but when he puts his

224 Dora Kalff, *Sandplay*.

brutal wars into the tray, they immediately become exposed to the light of consciousness.

Destruction in the tray such as Randy's explosions, dismemberment, and burning, or other activities chosen by the child, express a gradual, detailed transformation that usually occurs in the *nigredo* stage of the work. Spontaneous activities such as sifting, washing, pouring, burying and unburying, stacking and toppling, sorting, and for Randy, burning and warring, are deeply meaningful as aspects of a purifying process that has many alchemical terms. Work with the original psychic situation may include any of the operations based on the elements: *solutio* (water), *sublimatio* (air), *coagulatio* (earth), and the *calcinatio* (fire), that we see in Randy's trays.[225] These operations bring about the "volatilization of the stone," which we can understand as the purification, distillation, or organization into parts, of an unlivable situation. Volatilization symbolizes a spiritualization, a slow infusion of consciousness into the original unconscious situation, like heat into liquid. Consciousness gradually loosens the grip that the destructive energy holds on the personality. Unconsciousness is released, like steam or smoke. The material in the sandtray retort representing the unconscious situation is heated and washed, meditated upon, and worked, until it is released from the personality, becoming a less gripping phenomenon. The ego is compelled to perform these operations, expressions of the transformational process going on in the unconscious psyche.

Though sandplay activities may seem repetitive, especially in children, they are given as much free reign as possible without risking the child's safety. These outer activities reflect the inner psychic activity, the energic struggle that is engaged. As the unconscious energy transforms, the child's ego is loosened from its stagnant attachment to a complex. We see the initial state of the complex in early trays, and then we see a slow, session-by-session dismantlement of the complex. When the volatilization is complete, we see a shift towards creative activity, and the child becomes more involved in construction than destruction. If water is used for destruction or dissolution, water gradually becomes more an agent in creative work, and often the client turns to molding

225 Edinger's *Anatomy of the Psyche* details the psychological meaning of each of these operations.

and forming the sand in a *coagulatio* process. If fire is used, there is a turning point in which the fire becomes less destructive, and in every burning case I've seen, a shift in the work from fire to water indicates an important evolution toward creative work. The ego at this turning point becomes actively and spontaneously engaged in the individuality that springs like fresh water from the psychic center and is expressed in sandplay images.

Nigredo to Albedo

It is important to emphasize the fact that the dark psychological situation *itself* participates in the sandplayer's tranformation. Trying to eliminate Randy's hostility through behavioral modification alone would prohibit change on the elemental level, because the hostility and its energy would not be involved. Sandplay naturally provides a container into which a child's difficult psychological dynamics can be projected and transformed according to that child's inclinations. Dora Kalff's genius lay partly in her ability to follow the child's psyche, even through protracted periods of destructive work that can feel truly unholy, as it does with Randy. She trusted that the psyche's own healing urges would lead the child where he or she needed to go. When the complex is worked enough in the container, an inner path is cleared for healing and natural development. As Jung says, "the ever deeper descent into the unconscious suddenly becomes illumination from above."[226] Creative activity can be engaged, through which consciousness is re-experienced and the ego is strengthened, in relationship to the vivifying and organizing center of the conscious and unconscious personality, the Self.

One hallmark of this *enantiodromia* from destructive to creative work with the psyche is the mandala formation. The mandala heralds a renewal on the level of the Self as a result of ongoing contact with consciousness. And, mandalas indicate an ego experience, either current or incipient, of that renewal. The child who can create a mandala with a clear center is likely to feel more whole, more real, and basically good, as a result of contact with the healing and organizing capacity of the Self.

---

226   Jung, *Practice of Psychotherapy*, CW 16, ¶ 493.

Mandalas may appear in a series, or they may build from trays that show a gradual strengthening of a centering tendency from session to session.

Trays of a 5-year-old girl give us another example of *massa confusa* gradually organizing itself into a mandala formation. This girl was in danger of becoming selectively mute, stemming from a traumatic experience of violence. She did not speak during her first several sessions with me. The dark, confusing state of her inner experience is expressed in her initial tray (Figure 15) as chaos and overwhelm. Gradually, as she worked from session to session, the chaos became organized until she created a mounded mandala formation depicting the features of her own cat's face (Figure 16). She used parasols as ears, three oval stones as eyes and nose (the cat's left eye has a rubber band around it to signify the markings of the child's own cat). Both the chaotic and the organized trays contain the same blue parasol; in the second photograph it represents the cat's right ear. Although the cat's features are presented in detail, there is no mouth. We have a very clear image of the inability or unwillingness to speak, on a deep, animal level. By now the girl has been speaking, is having fewer temper tantrums, and she is dressing herself more consistently than when she began her therapy. The mandala shows some degree of separation from chaos. But the animal form and the lack of a mouth indicate there is more work to be done, strengthening her ability to speak for herself, in a humanized way. This mandala formation reflects a state in which the inner psychological situation has become more organized; development is now a possibility. A few sessions later the cat was again depicted as a mound, this time with a saxaphone representing its mouth. The saxaphone reflects the girl's new confidence in her ability to express herself on a feeling level.

A mandala formation that decidedly indicates a culmination of balanced wholeness and contact with the organizing principle of the Self we identify as a "Self tray." A Self tray expresses a tangible, numinous feeling of connection to the transpersonal center. Mandala formations, according to Jung, indicate the felt constellation of the Self as a protective force, and he wrote extensively about such mandala formations by his analysands.[227]

---

227 See especially "The Symbolism of the Mandala" in *Alchemical Studies*, CW 12.

Figures 15 and 16. Initial and later trays of a girl in danger of becoming selectively mute. The first tray displays the chaos of her original situation, the second a mandala formation several sessions later in the form of a cat's face (the two parasols are ears, oval stones below them eyes and nose). The stone circumference indicates a further impulse to establish a solid experience of being a reality in the world.

In his introduction to *The Secret of the Golden Flower,* he describes their meaning and function in the analytic process:

> When my patients produce these mandala pictures…[they] arise quite spontaneously, and from two sources. Once source is the unconscious, which spontaneously produces fantasies of this kind; the other is life, which, if lived with utter devotion, brings an intuition of the self, of one's own individual being. When the self finds expression in such drawings, the unconscious reacts by enforcing an attitude of devotion to life. For in complete agreement with the Eastern view, the mandala is not only a means of expression but also produces an effect. It reacts upon its maker. Age-old magical effects lie hidden in this symbol, for it is derived from the "protective circle" or "charmed circle," whose magic has been preserved in countless folk customs. It has the obvious purpose of drawing a *sulcus primigenius,* a magical furrow around the centre, the temple or *temenos* (sacred precinct), of the innermost personality, in order to prevent an "outflowing" or to guard by apotropaic means against distracting influences from outside. … Through the ritual action, attention and interest are led back to the inner, sacred precinct, which is the source and goal of the psyche and contains the unity of life and consciousness. The unity once possessed has been lost, and must now be found again.[228]

Whether for a child or an adult, the apotropaic influence that comes from engagement with the living center of the personality has an effect that can seem like magic. I often hear from parents and teachers when a child begins sandplay therapy that it seems to have worked like magic. There is an immediate influence on the child's ego, a result of even the initial contact with the living, inner core of the Self and therefore with the deepest truth of a psychological situation. At first the truth may be dark, but nevertheless it is the truth—and is allowed to be present as the truth, perhaps for the first time. Even in the initial dark stages of the work, the mandala has its beginning. Organization is initiated just by virtue of contact between the inner core of the psyche and the

---

228   Jung, *Commentary on "The Secret of the Golden Flower,"* CW 13, ¶ 36.

ego in its confused state. In the girl's trays above, we can see that the parasol used for the cat's ear was already present in her initial tray and is extracted later as a symbol for hearing as well as shelter. In Randy's first tray (Figure 2), a centering urge is visible, faint though it may be. If we look closely we see a kind of spiral, layers of a vague, circular formation constellating around the stone heart and the Empire State Building. The panther and the bear seem to be walking around the center, a circumam-bulation indicating that as threatening energies they are nevertheless in contact with the center of the personality, marked in this tray as a heart. The expression of such contact, especially so early in a process, is a posi-tive diagnostic indicator. In Randy's later trays we don't see a typically symmetrical mandala formation. But we do see the mandala take rudi-mentary shape in two forms: the ball of wax (Figure 14) and the temple (Figure 22), which is amplified in detail in Chapter 9. It is also possible that his very carefully organized battles, in which soldiers are lined up with equal numbers on both sides are mandala formations (Figure 25). Randy's provocative and numinous narrative in session 12, indicating he has discovered ancient wax and that he is king of the bloodfire, tell as much or more than the form of his tray, that he is having a new experi-ence of his individuality.

Alchemists describe the release of the stone from a contaminated influence as a mysterious, gradual, and thorough process, the details of which fill volumes. Fairy tales are concerned with the same dynamics. The minutia of the transformation process and its unending allegori-cal symbolism reflect how difficult it is to release consciousness from its unconscious fetters and to bring it into relationship with a greater sense of wholeness. The unending symbolism that the alchemists use to describe their experiences show us that while the stages of transfor-mation are similar, from one alchemist to the next, the contents of the transformation are unique to each alchemist. Likewise, the imagery and narratives involved in sandplay transformations are radically individual, even though each process encounters the hallmarks of transformational stages. With Randy's process as an example, we can see how important it is to pay close attention to the stages of transformation, the archetypal meaning of the images and narration, and the details of his individual symbolism.

In Randy's imaginal work, the appearance of Hades as the torturer who insists on suffering arrives as a climactic indication that suffering has indeed been recognized. Randy's suffering soul is being registered somewhere in consciousness. Paradoxically, Hades, the torturer, is also the purifier; this is a paradox that can be very difficult for consciousness to accept. The purified ash, the crown of the heart is the unlikely product of the Devil's torture and hell-fire. The retort of the sandtray has been the site of dismemberment by Hades, and now, is the site of resurrection of the king of the bloodfire. The new, relatively purified Randy who can adapt and achieve and make friends was always there, but through the burning process is gradually released from his unconscious burial in the hostile attitude and can be recognized and felt by consciousness as something completely new. The critical role that Hades plays in Randy's process shows us, in another way, how important it can be for the dark material to be acknowledged and creatively engaged.

Figure 17. Mercurius, crowned, emerges from the fire.

At this stage of the work in alchemy, the *prima materia* may appear as a crowned dragon, or a crowned Mercurius (Figure 17). Mercurius as a new king is encircled by fire and emerges from the fire in the alembic. Mercurius in this aspect of his incarnation is a spiritual phenomenon, separated from the "body" of the stone through volatilization. He is crowned because he has been connected to consciousness, and through this connection has transformed consciousness, bringing a new possibility.

The early release of the personality from an unconscious situation corresponds to the alchemical image of the soul released from a mortified body. An example is the *homunculus* in the *Rosarium Philosophorum* Picture 7 (Figure 18). The king and queen are dead, marking the death of an old union of conscious and unconscious energy. The essence of life, the soul, is released from the old, dead "body." In other words the old way, the old identification, is left for dead, marking an end to the *nigredo* and hence the onset of the *albedo* stage. In Buddhist terms, such a moment, when the ego is released from a way of identifying itself with a wound or a neurosis, marks an experience of "emptiness."

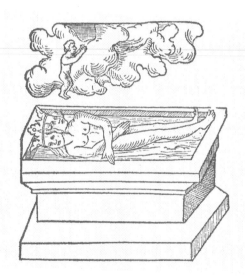

Figure 18. Ascent of the Soul. Homunculus personifying the soul extracted from the body and rising to join the spirit. The image of the homunculus points to an eventual birth of a new conscious attitude in the personality.

Randy's new release from the burned, melted, dismembered, and tortured complex of hostility is evident. He demonstrates a new kind of self-awareness, telling me he has new friends, and wondering if they come to see me. He is very proud to announce that he is the ball monitor in gym class. He tells me, "I'm in first grade doing third-grade math." He feels different, and the world feels different to him. The achievement is significant, but this is a delicate moment. His new state has not yet taken up permanent residence in his personality. Early on, the *albedo* can be experienced as a limbo state, and though much has been achieved, there is more work to be done.

For an adult, after working and working a contaminated attitude—a projection, a complex, a compulsion or addiction—the extraction of the soul out of the old way can be experienced in vastly different ways. In one sense, you may feel free of old illusions. In another, you may begin to feel a kind of death of the energy that once animated you, albeit in a neurotic way. The dragon or the complex is dismembered, at least in your cognitive understanding. There is clarity, but you are not quite reborn into a new way. When projection is being withdrawn, you live in a kind of white winter, in a limbo created by a relative loss of emotional attachment, even though with precious new knowledge. The soul in this *albedo* state is suspended, not in the body but hovering above. Jung wrote that the release from a certain level of identification and projection can even bring an experience of loss of soul,[229] and thus cause disorientation, despair, or hubris. Jung explains that "withdrawal of the naïve projections by which we have moulded both the reality around us and the image of our own character, we arrive at self-knowledge and an unveiled world."[230] A newly unveiled world can in one moment seem clear, and in the next feel foreign and colorless. It comes without the old emotional zing, however painful or illusory that zing may have been. If you are no longer fooled, no longer contained in a veil of illusion about yourself or another person or situation, you must come to terms with the new reality of the situation. You die to yourself, to the old ego reality, or perhaps you die to an identification with certain wounds. You might feel betrayed or let down, or even morally violated. A layer of unconscious perception is lifted, and this can shake your sense of reality. If a transference has been withdrawn, love itself may seem to be lost. Friendships may be re-evaluated. Your very fabric of relatedness seems suddenly rewoven, even though the preparatory work has gone on for months or years, or even decades.

229   Jung, *The Practice of Psychotherapy*, CW 16, ¶ 477.
230   Jung, *Mysterium Coniunctionis*, CW 14, ¶ 739.

In this crisis, it is especially important to understand how the unconscious is supporting you, and to glean from dream images what the psyche considers to be of value. Otherwise, without a larger perspective, the torment of being in limbo can be unendurable. Worse, you can slip into an inflation if you do not continue to work with the unconscious, thinking you are "cured." Jung emphasizes that the need for a symbolic perspective as opposed to intellectual theory, and the ability to understand dreams from a symbolic perspective is paramount.[231] Creative work is probably imperative because it keeps you face to face with your inner realities; it forces and expresses continuing development. Being open to the symbolic level of experience at this point can help keep Mercurius from falling back into his instinctual form and help prevent the complex or projection from recurring or moving into hubris (although it may take many attempts). What is needed is devotion to the process, a constant training on the Self, creative work with the psyche, and ethical devotion to life's demands. For a child like Randy, the work continues until he has fully integrated the change and has reached stable ground.

Albedo to Rubedo

There is no rule in alchemy, sandplay, nor analysis, for how long the *nigredo* lasts, how long purification takes, nor what a mandala looks like when the shift from *nigredo* to *albedo* begins. Randy's movement from black to white, like that of most people, is not clearcut and discrete; there is movement towards clarification, and then a return to old material to take care of things in a different way. But we do see a turning point arise in the new wax, ash, and the "king of the bloodfire." The moment of potential new life has been expressed. Now, we see Randy turn from the element of fire to the element of water. And importantly, we see him shift into play that is more creative than destructive. As this happens, Randy begins to express what the alchemists call the *rubedo* stage of the work, the reddening or coloring process that signals that a new state of consciousness is taking hold. Not only a mental situation, but a new felt reality is integrated into daily life; the clarity gained through cognitive insight is gradually worked into the felt body of the personality.

231   Jung, *The Practice of Psychotherapy*, CW 16, ¶¶ 479-80.

There is overlap between all three stages. For Randy we see movement into the *rubedo* begin with the discovery of the new reality in the red wax ("we are the haves, for once, we are the haves!") and then in the shift of his work from fire into water. He sprays and even floods the tray, kneading the sand and working the mud in an ongoing saturation process. Working with water helps Randy bring fully into his life the new consciousness developed through the purifying work with fire. Through this water stage, Randy seems to unite with the clarifying and refreshing quality of water thoroughly, and his new connection with his inner center becomes a renewing reality that is alive in him. In sandplay we try not to stop therapy until a constructive, adapted new attitude is clearly integrated into the child's life, and the personality has taken the "tincture" of the work. It is as if the personality has taken on new color and is connected to the flow of living meaning. As mentioned before, this connection in an adult is fostered through devotion to dreams, creative work, and active imagination in an ongoing relationship to the Self.

The stages of alchemical work are marked by different states of relationship between consciousness and the unconscious. There is an ongoing yearning on the part of the unconscious for relationship with consciousness, and vice versa, but the ego does not necessarily feel this in its original unity with the unconscious (Figure 8). A degree of separation between conscious and unconscious is achieved with the *albedo* stage; the soul is separated from the body and thus can be joined with the spirit. This is another way of saying that the original unconscious yearning (soul) can be separated from the personality and connected to a new level of conscious understanding (spirit), which then acts as a control. The *albedo* is marked by the first *coniunctio,* the mental union, called the *unio mentalis,* between the spirit and soul. The homunculus rises (Figure 17), symbolizing a level of soul consciousness achieved in understanding. The *rubedo* stage is marked by the second *coniunctio,* in which the soul and spirit are reunited with the body, pictured in the Rosarium images as the dew descending (Figure 19) to the mortified body, which is then renewed. This mortified body is the personality that lost its original way of being energized, lost its soul, through the consciousness-producing process of cleansing and purification. Now the soul returns and renews the personality with its own substance, which has been united with the spirit of understanding. In this state, relationship with the unconscious has been brought into life in a stable, felt sense, and relatedness, compassion, and discernment become stronger. Felt connection with the unconscious produces more than just a mental union; it forms a new attitude in the personality, a new way of being and relating in the world. Randy begins to experience a new attitude spontaneously; he becomes invested in friendships, he feels pride in his social and academic achievements instead of his bullying. Nevertheless he continues his work in the sandtray, and also purposefully engages in what he considers the incredibly frustrating handwork of origami, which is discussed later. He works instinctively to bring his new attitude thoroughly into his reality by confronting his frustration directly. It is clear at the end of his process that a change has been fully integrated into his personality. The second *coniunctio* is a kind of full-body saturation bringing a new way of life in which consciousness and the unconscious are in an ongoing, mutually renewing relationship to each other, rather than consciousness living in the grip of an unconscious attitude. A six-year-old does not have a conscious way of articulating this experience, but he does feel it, remarking for example that the world seems like a different place. For an adult, the second phase of the *coniunctio* is manifested in a transpersonal perspective that has gradually shifted from being a cognitive insight to a living, working reality, a way of life.

Moon Dust and the Unus Mundus

In the session after Randy's discovery of the wax, he tells me that during the past week, he went to the moon. "To the moon!" I say. "What happened?" He is reluctant to provide details, but declares, "I brought back the first handfuls of the moon's dust." Seeing his reluctance to elaborate, I simply say that it must have been quite an experience. He agrees, nodding his head like someone who has unveiled a world-changing secret of magnificent proportion. On a symbolic level as well, this fantasy is impressive. Randy is saying that he has gone into lunar consciousness and retrieved its substance. He is the first person to bring that substance back to the Earth.

The moon in antiquity and alchemy is that celestial body through which life on earth is funneled from the sun and the other planets, and is thus connected to *coagulatio* and incarnation; the moon is closely connected to the slow incarnation of plant life.[232] Moon dust in this sense would symbolize the miraculous, incarnating substance of Randy's true individuality as granted by the great mother. As a feminine entity, the moon and its substance acknowledge the cosmic value of Randy's individuality. The ability to value his own life—growing slowly like a plant in Randy—has felt very far away but is now available to him as a result of his lunar travel (his sandplay journey). His experience of moon dust is so much of a reality to him that he holds it in his hands, the way he held the ash in his hands. I imagine moon dust to be very similar to ash: both black and white, ethereal and material at the same time. This delicate substance is a wonderful symbol for the quality of the *albedo* that can arrive with a powerful insight, a full-blown illumination out of the darkness, and then disappear again in a moment if not incorporated into the feeling body. What was illuminating can become dark, and vice versa; you can have an experience of enlightenment, but until that experience is substantiated in life, holding onto it is like grabbing a fistful of slippery ash. In the black/white ash we see how *albedo* and *nigredo* are aspects of the same thing; their appearance in Randy's hands indicate their movement into the *rubedo* and integration into his personality. The truly healing nature of this fantasy, however, is that Randy has experienced a connection to the moon, a privilege that assures him the moon wants and even needs him to exist.

In the *albedo* stage the moon releases dew to revive the mortified body (Figure 19). The dew symbolizes the moistening quality of the psyche that saturates the personality with a renewing energy through the *rubedo* stage. The dew is the psychic substance, the symbol-forming function of the unconscious, that renews the personality on an ongoing basis. In "Psychology of the Transference," Jung writes of the dew:

---

232 The mysteries and profound symbolism of the moon cannot be fully expressed here. For more see Jung, "Luna," in *Mysterium Coniunctionis,* CW 14, beginning with ¶ 154.

After the ascent of the soul, with the body left behind in the darkness of death, there now comes an enantiodromia: the *nigredo* gives way to the *albedo*. The black or unconscious state that resulted from the union of opposites reaches the nadir and a change sets in. The falling dew signals resuscitation and a new light: the ever deeper descent into the unconscious suddenly becomes illumination from above. For, when the soul vanished at death, it was not lost; in that other world it formed the living counterpole to the state of death in this world. Its reappearance from above is already indicated by the dewy moisture. This dewiness partakes of the nature of the psyche ... (to freshen and animate), while on the other hand dew is synonymous with the *aqua permanens*, the *aqua sapientia*, which in turn signifies illumination through the realization of meaning. The preceding union of opposites has brought light, as always out of the darkness of night, and by this light it will be possible to see what the real meaning of that union was.[233]

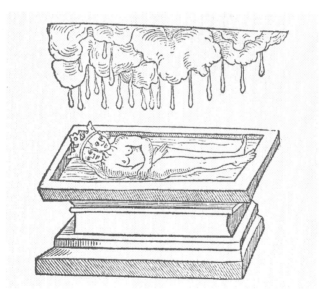

Figure 19. The dew descends into the mortified body and is a harbinger of the return of the purified soul. Jung refers to the dew as an experience of "illumination through realization of meaning."

233 Jung, *The Practice of Psychotherapy*, CW 16, ¶ 493.

Randy's fantasy tells me that, in conjunction with discovering new wax and identifying himself as the king of the bloodfire, he has had a profound experience of the moon in its vivifying capacity. As the one chosen to bring back the first of the moon's dust, he is elected for a cosmic task. Incarnating in him as a result of his archetypal journey in sandplay is a new, revived experience of his individuality, gotten by way of an encounter with the light that shines in the darkness. In his therapeutic process of working with the unconscious, its very substance has revived him. Pushing his violent urges back into the bath of the therapeutic container, he has extracted the soul that was "hidden" in the material of his violence, and that soul substance enlivens Randy's consciousness in a new way.

The "illumination through realization of meaning" emerges from dialogue with the unconscious, when suspension of an urge is engaged with the right meditative attitude. Illumination through meaning brings new energy to the deathlike experience of that suspension. When meaning emerges from the unconscious, you begin to feel your life stirring again, but with a less compulsive quality of energy. Meaning "saturates" the body or the personality with a renewed capacity to relate to oneself, others, and the world. The soul returns, but its yearning is more related to consciousness, and consciousness is more discerning about its choices.

Saying of his red ball of wax, "I remember it being black, not pink. But it was pink, not black," Randy seems to engage an unearthly source of information about his experience. He includes white in his perception of this red, sun-like image. We have to consider the ball of wax in its red aspect, as we have; it looks red, the way the sun is red in the morning. In one sense it harkens the dawning of a new emotional reality. But Randy refers to it as pink. That means for him it has some white in it, some moon, some soul, and purity. As a mixture of two pure colors, pink can symbolize either the contaminated, first version of the personality, the unconsciousness that has yet to be mortified, or (as in this case), pink can represent the new, revived union of red and white, of new life and a "whitened" realization, a combination of passion and consciousness. "Pink not black" is a mixture of the new life symbolized by the red sun and the soul-substance or "dust" of the white moon that Randy has collected. The bloodfire we can think of too as the essential nature of Randy's fascination with violence, his compulsion. That bloody essence, the drive itself, is now mixed with the wisdom of the moony aspect of the psyche, and Randy recognizes it as pink (not black, not in the dark of the unconscious). This specific mixture, passion and purity, especially by way of the moon, is the color of love, not passion. Randy's crude mandala, his ball of the new yet old wax, symbolizes Eros, from a transpersonal source, that Randy has re-discovered and brought to life on Earth as if he were the very first to do so. His is a world-creating experience.

Randy has become concerned about his grades, and he is coyly curious about the way people see him. He wonders if he can make more friends, and if his friends are loyal to him. His new social situation helps me realize that Randy is bringing a new feeling about himself into his life, or perhaps he has discovered something new that was there from the beginning and only covered up by hostility. He is willing to be vulnerable and concerned for others, a development on his feminine side. At the same time, his masculinity is tied more to achievement than violence.

However, there is still a significant sacrifice to be made, and in the next session we revisit *nigredo, albedo,* and *rubedo,* as if to review and solidify the movement through the stages via another iteration. We see again how the three stages are interwoven.

Chapter 9

BEST MAN IN THE ARMY:
SACRIFICE OF THE HOSTILE ATTITUDE

In the thirteenth session (Figure 20), another red candle is burned. As it lies in the sand smoldering and melting, Randy conducts a war in which "everyone is blown away, except for one guy." Some soldiers get stuck in the sand. Some fly through the flames. Randy asks several times if he can melt one of the soldiers, which are made of plastic. I resist; the fumes could be toxic. But Randy's persistence tells me that the burning of a soldier is important. I give in. By now I have invested in an air purifier. I repeat the mantra of rules that we have set down for burning. Randy holds the plastic soldier's head in the flames, watching it, enthralled as the head flames and melts, dripping into the sand. He presses the dis-integrating head into an enemy solider. One of the soldiers asks, "What happened? What the heck?" Randy continues the saga: "And then he was burned into history. He burned up. His wiener was burning up. He was such a good man, but he had to die."

Randy presses the man against the melted candle, and they meld together. Then he puts the solider back in the flames and continues to burn the body a little at a time.

"He's a very good man but he had to spend his only life dying for justice. And then a very bad thing happened. The light went out forever. He spent his life dying." Randy then takes the soldier's point of view, crying, "I only have a leg left. Let me die in peace!"

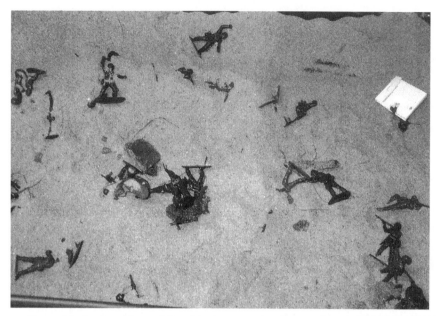

Figure 20. Session 13, a soldier, "the best man in the army" is sacrificed. His torso is lying melted in the sand; his legs are still intact. The melted wax is what remains of the candle over which the soldier was held.

Again Randy narrates, "He was the best man in the army. They placed his leg in a bottle. Someone [a woman] was crying really badly. He was her boyfriend." Later, when the soldier has been completely burned, Randy holds a female figure to the charred remains so she can kiss "all that is left of him."

As can happen in any individuation process, even though a new, unifying symbol like Randy's king, or his ball of wax, has emerged, marking a point of achievement and even indicating a certain level of completion in the *albedo* stage of transformation, aspects of the *nigredo* continue. Randy's process continues to illustrate how *nigredo* and *albedo* interlace with each other, and we could even say they are aspects of the same process, since there is always more blackness to whiten, and each confrontation with darkness informs the hard-won consciousness of the current level of development. As is emphasized again and again in alchemy, the "body," or the original level of psychological reality, must be completely mortified, the dragon absolutely dismembered—an experience in which ego consciousness reaches a level of humility that can grapple with the shadow and accept a mutually renewing relationship with the Self. Our consciousness is so strong and so sure of itself, that we must continually remember to sacrifice our tendency to "know" the truth as a matter of course. Thorough dismemberment of the ego's identification with an old attitude is very difficult to achieve because the Self is also being renewed. There always seem to be bits left over. We are speaking here of a goal that is closely tied to the wholeness that Jung describes as being out of reach and indescribable. The main element of dismemberment is the sacrifice of certainty, which Randy so clearly illustrates through the burning solider. We sacrifice certainty, and we sacrifice the position of the ego as the center of consciousness, realizing that there is a much more vast center, the Self, we cannot fully know. As a child, Randy needs to strengthen his ego for continued adaptation; what is sacrificed is the ego's identification with the certainty that hostility and violence are the right and only way. Again, this happens through volatilization, specifically the *sublimatio,* in which the violent urge goes up in the smoke of its own transformative fire—transformative because contained in a vessel and witnessed.

The death of a figure who "spent his only life dying for justice" is related to the divine child, the hero, and the alchemical king, sacrificed through dismemberment in order to be born again in a new form. The soldier melts and burns into oblivion like the "men burning yet alive" in Zosimos' vision, men who "become spirits by escaping from the body" through burning in boiling water.[223] This soldier is the inner man who suffers the torments of transformation and with whom Randy now has contact. He is the "best man in the army," that is, he is the one who can become more spiritual, and gain a new understanding. He is the arcane substance, the stone that can be, and is being, renewed. His death expresses the fate of a psychic content that lives for the purpose of dying, meaning that transformation is its main goal. Randy is experiencing the reality of this inner, living quality, whose mysterious transformation fuels the individuation process.

---

223   See Jung, "The Vision of Zosimos" in *Alchemical Studies*, CW 13. This quote is taken from Vision III, I, 3 and reappears in III, vi, 1.

In this dying and resurrecting aspect, the alchemical stone is associated with the symbol of Christ,[224] or other dying and resurrecting gods, or even, through the centuries, tribal chiefs who are sacrificed in order to renew the tribe.[225] A Christ-figure is the "best man in the army" of human beings because his sacrifice renews humanity. Christ was born to die—to sacrifice his earthly body and demonstrate the reality of the spiritual dimension. He renews the image of the Self as well as the human being. The feeling-tone of Randy's sacrifice in the fire was more reverent than most, as if Randy were experiencing on a more profound level what was dying in him, and what was coming to life as a result of the sacrifice. The transformation of the fighting energy takes place as the soldier literally goes up in smoke, his body slowly disappearing, volatilizing.

Edward Edinger discusses the sacrifice via fire as a *sublimatio* process that transforms the material realm into the heavenly realm, or the body into spirit:

> In early times fire was the chief method of sacrifice to the gods. Fire was thought of as a connecting link between the human and divine realms. That which was *sacrificed* by burning quite literally was "made sacred." That which is burned turns largely to smoke and ascends to the upper regions.[226]

Fire thus "purifies the things which are offered, liberates them from the bonds of matter," according to Iamblichus, meaning again that the original form of the "body," or the original pairing of conscious and unconscious contents, is gradually released, indicating the sacrifice. The smoky remains of unconscious material go to the upper regions, into the archetypal realm where they reclaim their godlike image. In an illustration from *De alchimia* (attributed to Thomas Aquinas) these spirits are personified as homunculi rising out of the body of a serpent (Figure 21). The homunculus here is another version of the *sublimatio* image of Mercurius rising out of the fire in the *vas* (Figure 17) and of the soul rising from the mortified king and queen in the *Rosarium* pictures (Fig-

---

224   See Jung, "The Lapis-Christ Parallel," *Psychology and Alchemy*, CW 12.
225   See Sir James Frazer, *Golden Bough* for a detailed history of the king sacrifice.
226   Edward Edinger, *Anatomy of the Psyche*, p. 38.

ure 18). The homunculus image is on the one hand the soul as we have discussed, leaving the confines of the unconscious complex. In another way the homunculus symbolizes the potential for a new, resurrected understanding or a reborn attitude in the personality—a consciousness that is like a newborn reality, released from the old way of seeing and yearning (the serpent or dragon) that is really completely dead.

Figure 21. Homunculi or personified spirits rising from the body of the serpent, from Aquinas' *De alchimia.*

In Randy's tray the soldier's girlfriend expresses a feeling realization that the fighting soldier, the best man in the army, has really died. She simply "kisses all that is left of him." It is one thing to die without a kiss, and quite another to die with one. As an inner phenomenon the kiss is a final goodbye to the body from the soul, indicating the death has been realized; the sacrifice and dismemberment is in a stage of completion because it is now truly felt. Yet, a kiss can also revive; it is a little *coniunctio,* a joining of opposites. As such, this kiss is another image for the soul or the dew descending to revive the dismembered dragon or the mortified body of the *Rosarium* couple (Figure 19). It is a kiss that says goodbye to one state, and hello to another.

As the expression of a feeling realization, the girlfriend's kiss in some small way parallels the lamentation of the Marys over Christ, or Isis over Osiris, or of any of the mythological women who through their tears and devotion realize the death of the dismembered god. These feminine figures are, via their intense realization of the god's death, instrumental in his resurrection. Likened to the soul that leaves and then returns to the old body, the lamenting feminine understands at a deep, feeling level what has passed, but she is also open to a new value. It is feeling that experiences the darkness, but also feeling that experiences the return of color to life after the darkness. In "Psychology of the Transference" Jung poignantly describes the turning point out of the *nigredo*, in which we might suffer a long period of darkness or loss of soul and then, when understanding can "contain those waters with the permanent water," a new feeling of life can emerge.

> Nobody who ever had any wits is in danger of losing them in the process, though there are people who never knew till then what their wits are for. In such a situation, understanding acts like a lifesaver. It integrates the unconscious, and gradually there comes into being a higher point of view where both conscious and unconscious are represented. It then proves that the invasion by the unconscious was rather like the flooding of the Nile: it increases the fertility of the land. The panegyric addressed by the *Rosarium* to this state is to be taken in that sense: "O natura benedicta et benedicta est tua operatio, quia de imperfecto facis perfectum cum vera putrefactione quae est nigra et obscura. Postea facis germinare novas res et diversas, cum tua viriditate facis diversos colores apparere." (O blessed Nature, blessed are thy works, for that thou makes the imperfect to be perfect through the true putrefaction, which is dark and black. Afterwards thou makest new and multitudinous things to grow, causing with thy verdure the many colors to appear.)[227]

Without the blackness of the "true putrefaction," the miracle of the "many colors" could not occur. The possibility of color returning to life arises from a position in consciousness that can integrate unconscious contents as natural, and not evil, phenomena. Psychological growth thus is realized as an achievement of nature, one that cannot be accomplished by will alone, but by willingness to participate with nature in a transformation designed by nature. The psyche is the thing that transforms, but depends on human consciousness to be understood and realized as such. Psyche is nature, as the alchemists seemed to experience. It is nature who takes us into the depths and nature who causes "the many colors to

227 Jung, *The Practice of Psychotherapy*, CW 16, ¶ 479.

appear" when we emerge with a potential new orientation in life. The ego's position sacrificed as the perceived center of the personality, once dismembered and relativized, can take the unconscious seriously. It is thus newly colored with ongoing contact with its transpersonal source. The many colors indicate the many feeling and thinking experiences that the personality can now integrate without being traumatized or threatened. As a result of participating in the dismemberment of its own unconscious state, the ego paradoxically becomes more substantial, able to relate to the unconscious and its many emotional and fantasy energies without being carried away by them.

In Randy's process we see how the living new attitude in *rubedo* begins to form as the *albedo* continues, perhaps even developing out of the *albedo* as it continues to be engaged. There are even times when *nigredo, albedo,* and *rubedo* seem to be happening simultaneously. In this tray, after the red sun has already appeared, a torture is endured, and a feeling realization takes place on a profound level. All these events are interdependent. We can pick out discrete aspects of each stage of the *opus* through their symbolism in this tray, and yet *in vivo* the stages are interdependent and cannot be separated.

For Randy, for any child of so young an age, the natural essence of psychological growth is readily observable because it results so immediately from contact with the inner world of natural images. It is chemical and spiritual. The "body" of the personality undergoes the same changes occurring in the retort of the sandtray, and the child might feel a shift in himself as a result. He does not realize that he is working with shadow or with *anima,* or with unconscious processes *per se*; he just knows that he is working with figures, sand, fire, or water. Any disorientation he may feel in this process may lead to a regression and get acted out in the world, even when the *rubedo* stage begins to appear. Repetition can be vitally important during this period of limbo: thus in Randy's process soldiers must be sacrificed even after the king of the bloodfire appears.

Whether child or adult, the psychological experience of an obsolete habit being tortured, dying, dismembered—that is, being suspended in the container of the imagination—leads to a resurrection—a transformation of libido, life energy. The energy is released from a chthonic or earthy form (physical, solid, locked into one way) to a more spiritual entity (free to engage in other forms). The sacrifice of the earthy aspect of the drive is emphasized in Randy's tray by the burning of the penis. In a six-year-old, such a transformation is not necessarily one aided by understanding, but more truly instinctual, chemical, and yet also psychic. The organ of the drive, is burning in the fire and being purified. The real sacrifice, voluntarily humbled in the torture of the sandplay, is Randy's containment in hostility. He has to let go of the hostility in order to grow.

Chapter 10

TEMPLE OF DOOM

In his fourteenth session (Figure 22) Randy completes his last burning. He melts another soldier and a candle, watching them intently as they mingle together in the sand. He burns a paper cube. He doesn't say much. He just watches, very quiet. There is no war.

In the sessions that follow Randy turns to water, which I have seen other children do after they finish burning, or between burning sessions. Sometimes he floods the tray, sometimes he uses mud to build things. From one session to the next he may flood the sand, mix it, mold it, and flood it again. I have plastic trays ready for this kind of work. The culmination of Randy's work with water occurs in his fifteenth session. Randy pours wet sand into a small glass bowl, then creates a mound on top of it. He says, "Now that's a temple!" He inverts the bowl into the sand to make a mound out of the entire bowl. He pours in lots of water, clearing the area around the mound. Then he turns the bowl right side up again and declares,

> "I'm going to make this as flat as a rock. As hard as a rock.
> Now I call this a pie. It's a masterpiece."

And after more work smoothing the top into a perfect dome shape, he announces,

> "It's called the mushroom. It's the temple of doom. Voila, I'm done."

Figure 22. Session 14, The "Temple of Doom," simple as it appears, represents
a mandala that joins the opposites.

A temple is "a building or a place dedicated to the worship or the presence of a deity."[223] When spelled with a capital "T" it is "any of the buildings in ancient Jerusalem dedicated to the worship of Jehovah." The temple is a place where ordinances are administered, as in the Mormon religion. Generally a temple is "anything considered to contain a divine presence." The word comes from the Latin *templum,* a sanctuary, or a space marked for observation by an augur.[224] Its Indo-European root is *tem-* "to cut." In its simplest form, a temple is a place cut out or reserved for contact with the divine, as in the Latin *templum,* "temple, shrine, open place for observations." And as an augury shelter a temple is a "place reserved or cut out," even a "small piece of timber," for the sake of consulting an oracle. In alchemy the *templum* is the head, the vessel in which the transformation of consciousness takes place. As a

223 Definitions from *American Heritage Dictionary of the English Language.*
224 An augur is a priest of divination, a seer or soothsayer. An augur can also be a sign, such as a rainbow or a black cat, that indicates good or bad luck for the future.

vessel of transformation the *templum* is also considered to be the *vas*.[225]
Making the temple as hard as a rock connects it with the rock of ages,
an image of God as a sheltering rock; the Dome of the Rock; or the rock
thought to mark the original Temple of Jerusalem. Even before history,
rocks have marked holy places on earth.

I was taken aback by this image, so different from anything that
Randy had done before (he has no religious affiliations). With his temple he announces that a sacred place has arrived. Taken symbolically
this temple refers to a holy place in Randy himself, a place where spiritualization takes place, where the personal and the transpersonal can be
joined in an ongoing relationship. His temple is made not with fire but
with earth and water, referring to Randy's earthy experience of himself.
The temple is Randy's own body, the temple of his soul. Or it is his soul,
as the vessel of his existence, which he now experiences in a new way, as
containing the reviving *aqua permanens* rather than torturous, burning
longing. If we think of Randy working the moisture of the dew of the
soul into the body of the psyche, then we have an image of the second
coniunctio, or at least an image for its aim. This temple of Randy's is his
own, earthy, muddy way of containing the divine, or being open to an
experience of the Self. The fact that this temple is made of mud indicates
a *coagulatio,* a birth of the transpersonal aspect in earthly reality, even
by way of the moon. He works the sand, flattening it and rounding it as
he creates his small temple. Its appearance is rudimentary, even though
he puts considerable effort into its creation. He forms and re-forms,
flattens and pounds, making it "hard as a rock," and again mounding
it over. The hardness connects this temple to the alchemical stone, its
roundness to the *templum.*

Yet Randy calls his creation the "temple of doom," acknowledging the
fact that the transpersonal aspect is not necessarily a positive experience
for the ego. To be doomed is to be sentenced to a horrible fate, death, or
the kind of destruction we have seen already in Randy's trays. The soldiers, fathers, sons, and innocent bystanders have been forced to suffer
and die. Their temple, the vessel of the sandtray and their transpersonal

---

225 See for example Jung, *Alchemical Studies*, CW 13, ¶ 89, and *Mysterium
Coniunctionis*, CW 14, ¶ 730.

reality as symbolized by the vessel, has been one of suffering for them, in the service of Randy's renewal.

From this development we can revisit the question: Is Randy's violence his fate, or the result of transgressions, or both? Randy's temple helps resolve this question without exactly answering it. Doom has a divine aspect, as has been felt and expressed throughout religious history as something visited on human beings by divine providence or an evil deity. Blame cannot really be assigned to the person experiencing the doom, because it can be something that occurs at the whim of the gods, as it did for Hercules, Odysseus, or Job. Randy's "doom" has already occurred; he was born into conflict and hostility, his own as well as his parents', although his situation has worsened by his acting out in violent activity. And yet doom in his tray is his transpersonal rock, in which refuge can be taken. The temple represents not only Randy's personal doom, but the whole arch of events, from doom to king, as an experience of being in the hands of the Self, and the mysterious workings of its opposite forces.

The idea of doom also connects Randy's temple to the prototypical form of the temple, which is a place "cut out" or reserved for the observation of an oracular event. Will there be good fortune or doom? One asks such a question from a place that is open to the divine aspect. Creating this temple, Randy has "cut out" such a place where fate, as heralded by the gods, can be experienced in the human realm. "Voila," he says, "Now that's a temple." There is a sense that, yes, this place right here is the place where the ego can have an experience of the Self, in both its positive and negative aspects. In the round *templum* of Randy's consciousness, this encounter has taken place and has transformed him. As is the head in alchemy, Randy's temple, his vessel, is a mandala. In a way his temple is the sand itself, and the containing tray. The temple of sandplay joins the opposites, good and evil, archetypal and personal, as experienced by Randy, and joins those unions to the archetypal dimension. I trust a "temple of doom" more than I would a temple of goodness and light, since it includes rather than excludes the influence of darkness and fiery conflict that have been fundamental to Randy's transformation.

Calling the temple a mushroom further stresses the importance of darkness and the feminine whose development has been so important in Randy's process. The mushroom, like the moon in his moon dust fantasy, and his bats (Chapter 10) grows in the dark, like a secret. It is a round and soft presence in contrast to the "hard rock" of the temple. It is nourished by the least valued aspect of life, the shit of life, and yet it develops its individual shape and size, unlike any other, and thrives. The mushroom is the thing that grows when you aren't looking, while you are working and working with the unconscious material. You turn around, and there is a light glowing in the dark, a moony shape coming out of the earth. You think it could not possibly have grown in the midst of all that shit and darkness, and yet, there it is, whole, and in some cases even edible.

Integration: Solutio

Randy's ongoing work with water is the process through which he integrates his transformed libido into his body (his temple), his life. Though fire and water are opposites, both symbolize the arcane substance. Water is as much a uroboric entity as fire. Both seek containment. But of the two, water is the superior container; fire cannot contain water. Fire is the drive, and especially emotional content, and water now comes forward as the drive control—the feeling capacity that, united with a new understanding or meaning, can contain the hostile emotion. Emotion always seeks a new container, specifically a human and humanizing container. Emotion wants relatedness, even though sometimes this desire is very hard to see. Randy's feeling for himself—his ability to relate to himself as a valuable human being and friend, this feeling capacity can act as a control now for violent reactions. As a reality in the world who can relate to others, he is less vulnerable to the explosive nature of his violent urges; he can contain most of them. He contains them partly through effort, but to an amazing extent he contains them with a natural ease, because he has changed.

Randy's work with the water seems to reflect the long process that can be required for a new attitude, and the moistening quality of soul-wisdom, to be truly integrated into the "body" as a working reality. I am speaking here of the body of the personality, symbolized by the alchemical body, the stone; but I am also talking to some extent about the concrete, material body. Randy has expressed his experience of himself as a temple, and I think he refers to his soul-vessel, but also the physical temple as the actual breathing shelter of his soul. Inversely, the temple is the transpersonal reality that he has encountered in sandplay, the free and sheltered space. Perhaps this temple has taken up shelter in Randy's nature, and he is expressing that experience in his own boyish way.

On a symbolic level the body refers to the unconscious, or the soul life of the personality. But also, children seem to experience their psychological changes in their physical bodies. I have seen often that the concrete body manifests the psychological change that comes from the transformed spirit. Children especially seem to change materially as the psyche is worked. Our temples are matter and they are psyche, and we would not have one without the other. We can no more deny the psyche in the body than we can the materiality of the psyche. Each is a living manifestation of the opposite poles of our reality, yet each unites those opposites in and of itself, if seen symbolically. We must be very careful, though, not to make the psyche concrete, and not to overly spiritualize the body. This is a mysterious realm where subtlety and details are very important on an individual level. In dream and other psychic images we see specific facts that describe a spectrum of relationship between body and psyche that we do not otherwise experience. Randy expresses through his temple of doom that his transformation is realized on the physical level as well as the psychic level, in the mysterious place where spirit and body meet.

Purification via torture has taken place for Randy mainly in the unconscious and therefore mainly in the physical body as his primary experience of himself. Although now he can articulate what anger does to him, he does not have a conscious view of the process he is going through. Working with water brings the process home, so to speak, integrating the new attitude into the working ego through the senses He seems to be working with the body of his psyche as much as the psyche of his body. This development and integration via the senses mimics the way a baby slowly emerges into consciousness via his or her senses.[226] Randy's process with water saturates his feeling of being in the world with the new possibility he has encountered in himself. He is slowly moistened with his new reality. As the sand over and over again is flushed, the new mental attitude born in Randy becomes integrated into the earth of everyday life.

The meaning of the *solutio* at this point has taken on a subtle shift; it is no longer a medium for washing and dissolving. Water is now a renewing solution, a mediator between body and soul, bringing them together in a second *coniunctio*. As dew that descends from heaven in the alchemical pictures, water is the soul, not in its original, yearning state, but as saturating wisdom (Figure 19). I have discussed the dew of the moon as the return of feeling that saturates the personality or breathes feeling (gold) into the body, coloring it with the realization that accompanies new consciousness. That feeling quality shifts now into wisdom, an experience of the *aqua mirifica*. The subtle difference between dew as feeling and dew as wisdom corresponds to the shift from the *albedo* to the *rubedo,* which, again, like all the alchemical stages, takes place on a continuum as much as a discrete changing of gears. In the *albedo* phase the personality is experiencing something so new that regression is a danger, as previously mentioned. When the world is newly unveiled from a certain formation of projection and identification, the loss of soul or loss of the old emotional involvement puts the personality in a fragile situation that requires devoted, ongoing work with the psyche. With the *rubedo* phase, the unveiling of the world is not so new, and the personality takes on a deeper level of substantiality as a result of yet further devotion to the inner work. Randy has been saturating his trays, indicating an infusion of the vivifying waters of wisdom. Each time this happens his new consciousness becomes more and more substantial, more real in the world. By the time he builds his Temple of Doom, Randy stands outside the violent complex in a more stable way and is less prone to falling back in. In an adult the realization that the old way

226 Irish sandplay therapist Agnes Bayley pioneered work with those unable to do sandplay because of early trauma and recognized the need to re-establish a basic sense of identity and security through work with the senses. I see this happening at any stage of development when a new way of being is in the world and needs to be anchored in the concrete body.

really is old can go on for many years. The old body continues to die as the new one resurrects, often very slowly. The resurrection requires ongoing development in the feeling realm, and when the resurrection is complete, wisdom comes alive as a quality that is highly resistant to emotional fire.

I had a dream while working with this material that seems to comment directly on the moistening quality of the *rubedo* phenomenon and the second *coniunctio*:

> *I receive a shipment of new clay. The new clay is dark brown and very moist. I put pieces of this clay into the round metal containers that hold my old clay, which is nearly dry, and greyish. Then I mix them together. I can feel with my fingers the wonderful moisture of the new clay and how it brings new life to the old clay. I squish the clay through my fingers and enjoy the pure sensation of mixing wet and dry together. This clay is called "play dough."*

Clay is the stuff from which the original human was made in many creation myths, and symbolically represents the basic material of life. Symbolic clay is both psyche and matter, the elemental opposites we are made of. We are psyche, but we are matter. Psychic images are mostly psyche, but they also have form, and we relate to their material form as well as their symbolic meaning if we take them seriously. Clay is the "stuff," the reality we work with in our dreams and active imagination, in meditation, in sandplay. It is the subtle body and the concrete body, and each is symbolically the other.

The new clay, the new psychic material, is rejuvenating, but the old clay is very important too. We have to have our original body, the old, complexed personality, as well as the concrete clay of the body itself, for a renewal to be felt. The brown color of the new clay compared to the grey color of the dry clay is also meaningful. Brown is closer to the earth, and related to nature; it contains a bit of red, the passion of life. Grey is a mixture of black and white, with no red, no life energy. The greyness or colorlessness would indicate a worn out connection to the renewing energy of the Self—there is no play in it. Since the dream occurred as a direct response to the contemplation of *rubedo,* we can hypothesize that this grey and dried-out quality is also an image of a stage of work that indicates purification, a clay that is dried of its original emotional content. The dry clay is parallel to the mortified body. The grey mortified body of the clay can be renewed by a new moist brown clay. The moistening is simultaneously a reddening process; as we receive wisdom, we become red with life and new energy. The rejuvenating water of meaning is experienced in a sensory way, not as intellectual understanding, and not as the lightning-spark of insight. Wisdom is not new, but feels new, and renews the old clay of our beings. The renewing water is in the body of the new clay, that is, in the psyche itself. The renewing of the clay thus is like a continuing body of dreams that can renew the personality, day by day. But such a renewal requires a personality that is conscious of receiving the meaning of the image, moist with the wisdom of the psyche.

Dream images can also renew a dry, stagnant, barren, or depressed state of mind. One of Jung's most beautiful statements regarding this phenomenon addresses the symbolism in the alchemical allegory, "*Introitus apertus,*" which challenges the philosopher to "moisten this dry earth with its own water." If dry earth symbolizes a lack of life energy, the moisture it needs come from the unconscious:

> If you will contemplate your lack of fantasy, of inspiration and inner aliveness, which you feel as sheer stagnation and a barren wilderness, and impregnate it with the interest born of alarm at your inner death, then something can take shape in you, for your inner emptiness conceals just as great a fulness if only you will allow it to penetrate into you. If you prove receptive to this "call of the wild," the longing for fulfilment will quicken the sterile wilderness of your soul as rain quickens the dry earth.[227]

The dream calls the mixed new and old clay "play dough," which would be the "stuff" of play, of the imagination, the basic material of the imaginal realm. As a mixture of the old and the new, this clay is the third reality born of the old consciousness and the new possibility. The dream seems to reiterate that imagination, play, is the stuff of renewal. The revitalizing of the play dough happens in everyday life, just

---

227 Jung, *Mysterium Coniunctionis*, CW 14, ¶ 190.

as play dough is an everyday kind of material. The dream testifies to the transformation that can happen through the everyday play of creative work, as in the "child's play" of alchemy, sandplay, dreamwork, or active imagination.

I could understand with this dream why the water that enlivens the alchemical mortified body is called dew from heaven. When a new way of being really arrives, unifying body, soul, and spirit, the experience is one of substance as well as grace and blessing, made all the more precious by the work that has gone before. You have worked hard for it, and yet it could not have arrived just because you wanted it. It is a change via the Self, by way of the moon, that you feel in your psychological bones, as it works its way into the marrow. Randy does not understand that he has been extracted from violence, but he has a realization in his being that he is a different person—a person with friends and self-respect. He has become more and more of an individual at the same time that he has become less and less tempted by violent urges. He is a substantial and more distinct human being, without having to articulate it any more than to announce that he is now at the top of his class in math. He feels the renewal in himself, and is living it.

The shift from *nigredo* to *albedo* to *rubedo* is difficult to pinpoint; in anyone's work it has threads that run from the very beginning to the very end of their work. In some alchemical texts the coloring of the *rubedo,* when new consciousness is integrated into life, is closely associated with the *albedo* and no differentiation is made. Randy works on both levels: the water has a purifying quality, but also a penetrating one, and accompanies his ability to bring his newly won sense of himself into his everyday life, into small activities and play. For example, in his final three sessions Randy struggles with origami. He gets frustrated with the "stupid" instructions and with the limitations of his own hands in the folding process, but he endures. He works through his frustration and ends up with a cube, a kite, and a pelican. Randy's work with origami, in which he challenges himself to work through frustration rather than erupt, helps bring his new spirit or "force field" fully into his being. He literally exercises his tolerance during this time, proving to himself that he can contain his frustration (suspend the urge) and not explode. If he experiences insight or wisdom, I would say this occurs in his relative acceptance of the fact that simple tasks such as folding paper or following instructions can be enormously frustrating, but that this frustration is part of life. He has to some extent given up an attachment to things going his way, or being easy. In his own small way, Randy through this process is re-integrating the energy of his own anger. His new consciousness and new ability to feel for himself are uniting with the experience of frustration, and he is not exploding.

The New Hermaphrodite

The mounded image of the temple or mushroom, looking somewhat like a pregnant belly, announced the presence of a new reality related to Randy's individual experience but also connected to a divine presence that psychologically we can consider the Self. As a "temple of doom," this image integrates the opposites, as any mandala does, reflecting the paradoxical nature of the Self as a *complexio oppositorum*. The temple of doom brings together Randy's positive and negative experiences, and indicates that his hostility is now contained in the whole picture of Randy. Anger is part of the whole rather than a split-off, contaminating energy. Underlying this integration is the union of masculine and feminine aspects in Randy, which slowly have become more related to each other. Randy's work has brought into existence a new coupling of feeling and understanding. These new alliances, requisite of any psychological transformation, are symbolized in alchemy by the new, crowned hermaphrodite (Figures 23 and 24). As Jung says, "These images are naturally only anticipations of a wholeness which is, in principle, always just beyond our reach."[228] We can experience new degrees of wholeness, as Randy experiences a new reality in himself, but wholeness is always relative.

At this stage in Randy's work, I would like to return to a strange and wonderful fantasy that he told me in his third session, after he conducted the war of the ancient dragon. It is a great secret, one that seems to have been forming for a while. He finds the courage to tell me, cautioning that I must swear to keep the secret from his mother. I promise. He tells

---

228   Jung, *Practice of Psychotherapy*, CW 16, ¶ 536

Figure 23. The new, crowned hermaphrodite Jung refers to as a "hybrid thing" that reflects the "anticipation of wholeness" that is "always just beyond our reach."

me that his house is "as wide as the school and twice as high," and has a lot of secret passageways, where bats nest. He is responsible, he says, for cleaning up the eggshells that fall out of the rafters when the bats hatch out of their eggs. Mom doesn't know about the bats, but she sees the eggshells and pays him ten dollars a day to clean them up. He describes the passageways and the bats extensively, as if they really do exist.

On a symbolic level, Randy is telling me that he has intimate, secret knowledge of new life that is born in the rafters, so to say, or in the unconscious area above the head. The bats indicate a primitive, featherless development in the spiritual realm: a drive for a continuous birth of new consciousness that can fly, but only in the dark of the unconscious. Bats do not lay eggs, of course; they are mammals. Randy experiences the eggs and shells as material evidence of a birth process, and this materiality indicates how strongly the birth process is working in him, how real it is. It is tempting to call this fantasy a vision. He sees and touches the shells from which the baby bats emerge, and this happens every day. He is responsible for cleaning up those shells, and this means he is engaged in the process and feels dutiful about it. This birth process symbolizes creative activity in Randy's psyche, an inner urge to give birth that stands in direct opposition to the destructive, warlike urges. The urge for something new to get born is so strong that it generates a tactile experience for Randy, putting him in direct contact with the psychic process. In other words, through his fantasy he encounters the "realm of the subtle bodies" in which an inner psychic process and the outer world of matter come together to produce an image and an experience of birth. When we realize the depth and intensity of Randy's experience, we get a clear picture of the healing potential available to him; he is engaging in the creative, perpetually birthing energy in the unconscious. Through these fantasies, the unconscious provides a healing antidote to Randy's hostility and points toward the new life available to him.

Randy's birthing bats symbolize an incipient individuation instinct. There is the possibility, according to this fantasy, of getting out of the egg, which is the original unconscious experience. In the fantasy his own mother pays him, or acknowledges the value of his participation in the birth process, even though his mother in the outer world doesn't know anything about it. In this seeming conflict is the experience of two levels of consciousness. In the fantasy Randy's personal mother pays him, but behind her stands the great mother, the one who generates life and images of birth. Randy realizes that in the world of conscious reality, his own mother does not know what is going on and would not understand if he told her. He doesn't want me to tell his mother either. If I take the fantasy seriously as a psychic fact and realize its meaning, I suffer no ethical dilemma entering this secret pact and taking it as a reality. He knows—or his psyche knows—that I will understand the delicate nature of this fantasy and its need for secrecy in order to have an effect. Bringing this precious fantasy into the light of day where it would not be believed would destroy it and Randy's relationship with it. On a daily basis, Randy tells me, he cleans up those shells, and the great mother gives him money, which symbolizes valuable energy, in return for his devotion. Individuation promotes birth on a daily basis as long as we attend to that birth as a psychic reality. If nothing else, the fantasy tells me that Randy's psyche is fully engaged in his therapy. By the time he fights the war of the ancient dragon, he is engaged with the great mother in a secret healing mission.

Bats come with a wealth of associations in world mythology. Bats in the Far East are associated with good luck, in Mexico with death. Among the Pueblo Indians they are harbingers of rain. They are related to vampires in many cultures. In Africa, bats represent clear sight because of their ability to see at night. In Taoist tradition they are associated with the "fortifying of the head" because the weight of the bat's brain relative to the rest of its body forces it to roost upside down. The bat is the only flying animal to suckle its young, and for this reason is associated with prolific birth and the nourishing aspect of motherhood. The bat accompanies Artemis in her guise as protector of childbirth and infancy.

According to the Native American Medicine Cards, the bat is a symbol for reincarnation and is revered as such by the Aztec, Toltec, Toucan, and Mayan nations. Reincarnation for these cultures refers not only to physical rebirth after death but also the rebirth of the personality through new patterns of behavior and attitudes, dying to the old and being born to the new, as occurs in Shamanistic rituals. The hanging upside down symbolizes the ability to turn oneself upside down and become a newborn being.[229] This is the meaning that seems closest to Randy's bats. They are pushing on a daily basis for Randy's own rebirth.

The bat's association with birth and regeneration may be connected to fact that the alchemical hermaphrodite is often pictured with bat wings (Figures 23 and 24). The bat wings of the new, crowned hermaphrodite (pictured) are vestiges of the original form of the hermaphrodite out of which the new one has been produced. They are the wings of the

---

229   J. Sams, D. Carson, and A. Werneke, *Medicine Cards: The Discovery of Power Through the Ways of Animals with Cards.*

original dragon, or the uroboric reality out of which arises new psychic development, a new, crowned reality.

Figure 24. Crowned hermaphrodite with bat wings. This is an image of the *coniunctio*, the integration of opposites that occurs at the end of the work. The bat wings are vestiges of the original *prima materia*.

Randy's array of sandplay images, so gritty and paradoxical, are similar in their small ways to the new hermaphrodite. My fondness for the images and story in Randy's trays, besides the fact that they do anticipate that wholeness that is just beyond our reach, is their salty ingenuousness in doing so. They are wonderful and strange, divine and yet

crude in the most boyish way imaginable. They are completely natural.
In these ways too they resemble the strange newborn hermaphrodite,
the product of an equally natural imagination completely absorbed in
the workings of the fire, the water, the mud, and the gore. Jung says of
this "hybrid thing:"

> Whereas the Christian figures [occurring in that day] are the
> product of spirit, light, and good, the alchemical figures are
> creatures of night, darkness, poison, and evil. These dark ori-
> gins do much to explain the misshapen hermaphrodite, but
> they do not explain everything. The crude, embryonic fea-
> tures of this symbol express the immaturity of the alchemist's
> mind, which was not sufficiently developed in two senses:
> firstly he did not understand the real nature of chemical com-
> binations, and secondly he knew nothing about the psycho-
> logical problem of projection and the unconscious. All this
> lay as yet hidden in the womb of the future.[230]

Jung's observation that the "immaturity of the alchemist's mind"
could participate so poignantly in the archetypal reality of transformation helps me take faith in the crude, natural images of Randy's
transformation. His six-year-old imagination is equally as naïve as the
alchemists', and he is equally fascinated and changed by the projected
workings of his mind. Randy's new attitude towards himself, his friends,
and his life is born out of the darkness, poison, and even the evil nature
of an ancient dragon, war, and fire. His images arise out of the unso-
phisticated earth of his own psyche and the energy he works with. He is
no saint; he is still very much a mischievous little boy. His true nature
has not been manipulated. Rather, out of the dark matter of his hostility
and his very natural engagement in that darkness, a bit of compassion
has arrived, a relatedness that contributes in its own small way to the
soul of the world.

---

230   Jung, *The Practice of Psychotherapy,* CW 16, ¶ 533.

Chapter 11

FORCE FIELD: A LIVING SPIRIT

Figure 25. In his later sessions, Randy's wars become more organized, and soldiers are carefully counted and lined up with equal numbers of good guys and bad guys on each side. These careful formations could be considered mandalas. They demonstrate how the new way of being is made of the same "material" (the fighting soldier) as the old way of being, even though the fighting energy has been transformed.

During the next several sessions, Randy continues to test his limits and mine as we do projects together and play games. He cheats to win, and we talk about cheating (pride is another form of fire). He does his work with origami, challenging himself to deal with inevitable frustration. He wants to keep trying, wants to stick with an activity even though it makes him angry, just to see if he can do it. He can. We talk about what it feels like to get angry, and we discuss anger philosophically. He points out how it can take over your body and even your mind.

Playing games and losing some interest in sandplay is evidence that the intense operations in the sandplay work are coming to completion. He wages a few more wars in the sandtray, but they are quite organized (Figure 25). He counts the soldiers and arranges them carefully to make sure there are an equal number on each side. This careful organization and order indicates that the internal conflict has become more organized; this is evident in Randy's behavior and attitude, his pride in his friends and schoolwork.

In his twenty-first session (Figure 26, Randy builds a construction out of yellow paper and stands it up on the table, a tall, rectangular accordion shape. Soldiers shooting at bad guys take shelter behind it. He calls it a force field. It "protects the good guys" by giving them "extra power." I ask Randy if the good guys always win. He says, "No, sometimes the bad guys win." But for this war, the good guys have the force field on their side. "It gives them extra protection and makes them really smart."

Figure 26. A protective force field, quite large in proportion to the soldier.

The force field that protected the baby from the fire in session 11 has reappeared. Randy not only speaks about it but also creates this force field, bringing it into reality and making it gigantic in proportion to the soldiers it protects. As a living energy (as described in Chapter 5), the force field is protective and even discerning, on the side of the good guys. As an inner energy in Randy, it feels quite different from the chthonic and destructive energy of the original violence that once drove Randy. This force field helps Randy distinguish between the creative and destructive energies in himself, certainly to a much greater extent than when he first started therapy. He is now identified with the good guys and wants them to win. He wants to win. He wants the good guy in him to win, to keep his new friends and his status as a good student. The protective, discerning energy he feels is nothing less than his own inner sense of basic goodness, which has been redeemed out of the original fire and war. Randy's force field is akin to the resurrected *lapis,* a redeemed (volatilized) form of libido. This life energy lives in Randy now as a newly experienced, individual and individuating spirit. His fire is a new fire, and he is changed by that fire.

The transformation of the fire-energy itself, from a destructive drive to a protective force, brings Randy an experience of himself as someone who fights the good fight, a fight that is not self-destructive but pushes for creative work and the natural childhood work of individuation. Randy's experience of himself as a person who can live with anger rather than be taken over by it has been brought about by the elemental transformation of fire, a form of life energy. Jung points out that in alchemical texts the new king, the *filius regius,* is identical to the "warrior fire," both heroic, personified versions of the transformed *lapis*:

> In *Ars Chemica* we encounter the *Rex coronatus* and *filius noster rex genitus,* of whom it is said: "For the son is a blessing and possesses wisdom. Come hither, ye sons of the wise, and let us be glad and rejoice, for death is overcome, and the son reigns; he is clothed with the red garment, and the purple [*chermes*] is put on." He lives from "our fire," and nature "nourishes him who shall endure for ever" with a "small fire." When the son is brought to life by the opus, he becomes a "warrior fire" or a "fighter of fire."[223]

"Brought to life by the opus," Randy's renewed sense of self, his small fire, is nourished by nature, and will endure.

---

223 Jung, *Alchemical Studies,* CW 13, ¶ 184.

ABOUT THE AUTHOR

Laurel Howe is a Jungian analyst who earned her diploma from the Centre for Research and Training in Depth Psychology According to C.G. Jung and Marie-Louise von Franz, Zürich. She is a faculty member of the C.G. Jung Institute of Colorado, a teaching member of the International Society of Sandplay Therapy and the Sandplay Therapists of America, and an advisory board member of the Colorado Sandplay Therapy Association. She has a private practice in Lakewood, Colorado where she works with children and adults and mentors students of analytic psychotherapy and sandplay therapy. In addition to sandplay and alchemy, Laurel writes and presents lectures on the history and psychological meaning of Mary Magdalene and feminine archeological images from the Levant prior to and during the development of the Old Testament.

BIBLIOGRAPHY

American Heritage Dictionary of the English Language. Boston, etc.: Houghton Mifflin, 1981.

Abt, Theodor. *Book of the Explanation of the Symbols Kitāb Hall ar-Rumūz by Muhammad ibn Umail. Corpus Alchemicum Arabicum, Vols. I, IA, and IB.* Zürich: Living Human Heritage, 2009.

Amman, Ruth. *Healing and Transformation in Sandplay: Creative Processes Made Visible.* Peru, Illinois, Open Court Publishing, 1991.

Bradway, Kay, and McCoard, B. *Sandplay: Silent Workshop of the Psyche.* New York: Routledge, 1997.

Edinger, Edward F. *Anatomy of the Psyche: Alchemical Symbolism in Psychotherapy.* La Salle: Open Court, 1985.

_____. *Ego and Archetype.* Pelican Books, 1969.

Frazer, Sir James George. *Golden Bough: A Study of Magic and Religion.* New York: Mentor Books, 1964.

Jung, Carl Gustav. *Alchemical Studies.* Collected Works of C.G. Jung, Vol. 13. Princeton University Press, 1967.

_____. *Memories, Dreams, Reflections.* New York: Vintage Books, 1965.

_____. *Mysterium Coniunctionis.* Collected Works of C.G. Jung, Vol. 14. Princeton University Press, 1970.

_____. *Psychology and Alchemy.* Collected Works of C.G. Jung, Vol. 12. Princeton University Press, 1968.

_____. *The Practice of Psychotherapy.* Collected Works of C.G. Jung, Vol. 16. Princeton University Press, 1954.

_____. *The Structure and Dynamics of the Psyche.* Collected Works of C.G. Jung, Vol. 8. Princeton University Press. 1960.

_____. *Symbols of Transformation.* Collected Works of C.G. Jung, Vol. 5. Princeton University Press, 1956.

_____. *The Red Book: Liber Novus.* New York: W.W. Norton & Co, 2009.

Kalff, Dora. *Sandplay: A Psychotherapeutic Approach to the Psyche.* Santa Monica: Sigo Press, 1981.

_____. *Sandspiel: Seine Therapeutische Wirking auf die Psyche.* Zürich: Eugen Rentsch Verlag, 1979.

Neumann, Erich. *The Origins and History of Conscious.* Princeton: Bollingen, 1970.

_____. *The Child.* Boston: Shambhala, 1990.

Sams, J., Carson, D., and Werneke, A. 1999. *Medicine Cards: The Discovery of Power Through the Ways of Animals with Cards.* New York: St. Martin's Press, 1999.

Trismosin, Solomon. *Splendor Solis.* London: Kegan Paul, Trench, Trubner & Co., Ltd., 1582, reprinted 2003.

Turner, B. *The Handbook of Sandplay Therapy.* Cloverdale, California: Temenos Press, 2005.

Von Franz, Marie-Louise. *Alchemy: An Introduction to the Symbolism and the Psychology.* Toronto: Inner City Books, 1980.

_____. *Problems of the Feminine in Fairy Tales.* Dallas: Spring Publications, 1972.

_____. *Psyche and Matter.* Boston and London: Shambhala, 1992.

Whitney, Mark, dir. *Matter of Heart* (film). Copyright 1983, Jung Institute of Los Angeles, 1985.

INDEX

You might also enjoy reading:

Marked By Fire: Stories of the Jungian Way edited by Patricia Damery & Naomi Ruth Lowinsky, 1ˢᵗ Ed., Trade Paperback, 180pp, Biblio., 2012 — ISBN 978-1-926715-68-1

The Dream and Its Amplification edited by Erel Shalit & Nancy Swift Furlotti, 1ˢᵗ Ed., Trade Paperback, 180pp, Biblio., 2013 — ISBN 978-1-926715-89-6

Shared Realities: Participation Mystique and Beyond edited by Mark Windborn, 1ˢᵗ Ed., Trade Paperback, 270pp, Index, Biblio., 2014 — ISBN 978-1-77169-009-6

Pierre Teilhard de Chardin and C.G. Jung: Side by Side edited by Fred Gustafson, 1ˢᵗ Ed., Trade Paperback, 270pp, Index, Biblio., 2014 — ISBN 978-1-77169-014-0

Re-Imagining Mary: A Journey Through Art to the Feminine Self by Mariann Burke, 1ˢᵗ Ed., Trade Paperback, 180pp, Index, Biblio., 2009 — ISBN 978-0-9810344-1-6

Advent and Psychic Birth by Mariann Burke, Revised Ed., Trade Paperback, 170pp, 2014 — ISBN 978-1-926715-99-5

Transforming Body and Soul by Steven Galipeau, Rev. Ed., Trade Paperback, 180pp, Index, Biblio., 2011 — ISBN 978-1-926715-62-9

Lifting the Veil: Revealing the Other Side by Fred Gustafson & Jane Kamerling, 1ˢᵗ Ed., Trade Paperback, 170pp, Biblio., 2012 — ISBN 978-1-926715-75-9

Resurrecting the Unicorn: Masculinity in the 21ˢᵗ Century by Bud Harris, Rev. Ed., Trade Paperback, 300pp, Index, Biblio., 2009 — ISBN 978-0-9810344-0-9

The Father Quest: Rediscovering an Elemental Force by Bud Harris, Reprint, Trade Paperback, 180pp, Index, Biblio., 2009 — ISBN 978-0-9810344-9-2

Like Gold Through Fire: The Transforming Power of Suffering by Massimilla & Bud Harris, Reprint, Trade Paperback, 150pp, Index, Biblio., 2009 — ISBN 978-0-9810344-5-4

The Art of Love: The Craft of Relationship by Massimilla and Bud Harris, 1st Ed., Trade Paperback, 150pp, 2010 — ISBN 978-1-926715-02-5

Divine Madness: Archetypes of Romantic Love by John R. Haule, Rev. Ed., Trade Paperback, 282pp, Index, Biblio., 2010 — ISBN 978-1-926715-04-9

Tantra and Erotic Trance in 2 volumes by John R. Haule

  Volume 1 - Outer Work, 1st Ed., Trade Paperback, 215pp, Index, Bibliography, 2012 — ISBN 978-0-9776076-8-6

  Volume 2 - Inner Work, 1st Ed., Trade Paperback, 215pp, Index, Bibliography, 2012 — ISBN 978-0-9776076-9-3

Eros and the Shattering Gaze: Transcending Narcissism
by Ken Kimmel, 1st Ed., Trade Paperback, 310pp, Index, Biblio., 2011 — ISBN 978-1-926715-49-0

The Sister From Below: When the Muse Gets Her Way
by Naomi Ruth Lowinsky, 1st Ed., Trade Paperback, 248pp, Index, Biblio., 2009 — ISBN 978-0-9810344-2-3

The Motherline: Every Woman's Journey to Find Her Female Roots
by Naomi Ruth Lowinsky, Reprint, Trade Paperback, 252pp, Index, Biblio., 2009 — ISBN 978-0-9810344-6-1

The Dairy Farmer's Guide to the Universe in 4 volumes
by Dennis L. Merritt:

  Volume 1 - Jung and Ecopsychology, 1st Ed., Trade Paperback, 242pp, Index, Biblio., 2011 — ISBN 978-1-926715-42-1

  Volume 2 - The Cry of Merlin: Jung the Prototypical Ecopsychologist, 1st Ed., Trade Paperback, 204pp, Index, Biblio., 2012 — ISBN 978-1-926715-43-8

  Volume 3 - Hermes, Ecopsychology, and Complexity Theory, 1st Ed., Trade Paperback, 228pp, Index, Biblio., 2012 — ISBN 978-1-926715-44-5

  Volume 4 - Land, Weather, Seasons, Insects: An Archetypal View, 1st Ed., Trade Paperback, 134pp, Index, Biblio., 2012 — ISBN 978-1-926715-45-2

Four Eternal Women: Toni Wolff Revisited—A Study In Opposites
by Mary Dian Molton & Lucy Anne Sikes, 1st Ed., 320pp, Index, Biblio., 2011 — ISBN 978-1-926715-31-5

Becoming: An Introduction to Jung's Concept of Individuation
by Deldon Anne McNeely, 1st Ed., Trade Paperback, 230pp, Index, Biblio., 2010 — ISBN 978-1-926715-12-4

Animus Aeternus: Exploring the Inner Masculine by Deldon Anne McNeely, Reprint, Trade Paperback, 196pp, Index, Biblio., 2011 — ISBN 978-1-926715-37-7

Mercury Rising: Women, Evil, and the Trickster Gods
by Deldon Anne McNeely, Revised, Trade Paperback, 200pp, Index, Biblio., 2011 — ISBN 978-1-926715-54-4

Gathering the Light: A Jungian View of Meditation
by V. Walter Odajnyk, Revised Ed., Trade Paperback, 264pp, Index, Biblio.,
2011 — ISBN 978-1-926715-55-1

The Promiscuity Papers
by Matjaz Regovec, 1ˢᵗ Ed., Trade Paperback, 86pp, Index, Biblio., 2011
— ISBN 978-1-926715-38-4

Enemy, Cripple, Beggar: Shadows in the Hero's Path
by Erel Shalit, 1ˢᵗ Ed., Trade Paperback, 248pp, Index, Biblio., 2008
— ISBN 978-0-9776076-7-9

The Cycle of Life: Themes and Tales of the Journey
by Erel Shalit, 1ˢᵗ Ed., Trade Paperback, 210pp, Index, Biblio., 2011
— ISBN 978-1-926715-50-6

The Hero and His Shadow
by Erel Shalit, Revised Ed., Trade Paperback, 208pp, Index, Biblio., 2012
— ISBN 978-1-926715-69-8

Riting Myth, Mythic Writing: Plotting Your Personal Story
by Dennis Patrick Slattery, Trade Paperback, 220 pp. Biblio., 2012
— ISBN 978-1-926715-77-3

The Guilt Cure
by Nancy Carter Pennington & Lawrence H. Staples, 1ˢᵗ Ed., Trade
Paperback, 200pp, Index, Biblio., 2011 — ISBN 978-1-926715-53-7

Guilt with a Twist: The Promethean Way
by Lawrence Staples,1ˢᵗ Ed., Trade Paperback, 256pp, Index, Biblio., 2008
— ISBN 978-0-9776076-4-8

The Creative Soul: Art and the Quest for Wholeness
by Lawrence Staples, 1ˢᵗ Ed., Trade Paperback, 100pp, Index, Biblio., 2009
— ISBN 978-0-9810344-4-7

Deep Blues: Human Soundscapes for the Archetypal Journey
by Mark Winborn, 1ˢᵗ Ed., Trade Paperback, 130pp, Index, Biblio., 2011
— ISBN 978-1-926715-52-0

Phone Orders Welcomed
Credit Cards Accepted
In Canada & the U.S. call 1-800-228-9316
International call +1-831-238-7799
www.fisherkingpress.com

Printed in Great Britain
by Amazon